WHAT IS
RHETORICAL
THEOLOGY?

D1397604

WHAT IS RHETORICAL THEOLOGY?

Textual Practice and Public Discourse

DON H. COMPIER

WAGGONER LIBRARY
DISCARD

TRINITY PRESS INTERNATIONAL
Harrisburg, Pennsylvania

MACKEY LIBRARY
Trevecca Nazarene University

Copyright © 1999 by Don H. Compier

All rights reserved. No part of this book may be reproduced, stored in a retrieval system, or transmitted, in any form or by any means, electronic, mechanical, photocopying, recording, or otherwise, without the written permission of the publisher.

Trinity Press International, P.O. Box 1321, Harrisburg, PA 17105
Trinity Press International is a division of the Morehouse Group.

Cover design: Dana Jackson
Cover art: *School of Athens* by Raphael, Vatican Museums & Galleries, Rome/Fratelli Alinari/SuperStock

Library of Congress Cataloging-in-Publication Data
Compier, Don H.
    What is rhetorical theology? : textual practice and public discourse / Don H. Compier.
        p.   cm.
    Includes bibliographical references and index.
    ISBN 1-56338-290-3 (pbk. : alk. paper)
    1. Rhetoric – Religious aspects – Christianity. 2. Theology – Methodology.   I. Title.
    BR115.R55C66   1999
    230′.01 – dc21   99-33833

Printed in the United States of America

99   00   01   02   03   04   10 9   8   7   6   5   4   3   2   1

Contents

Preface

These are interesting times for the discipline variously known as dogmatics, systematic theology, or constructive theology. In fact, observers from other fields of study might well ask whether there is sufficient coherence to speak of a single discipline. In recent decades we have witnessed the emergence of very different approaches to the theological task, pursuing diverse ends through the employment of a plethora of methods, doctrinal foci, and conversations with related disciplines.[1]

In some quarters this situation has rung bells of alarm. Significant practitioners of the theological discipline(s) lament the breakdown of consensus and the seeming inability to agree on a common program of research and teaching, with unfortunate results for church and society.[2] Others, including this writer, tend to view the state of theology in more positive terms, evaluating the current "fragmentation" as the inevitable and welcome result of the emergence of new theological voices.[3] Even so, theology's declining ability to attract the attention of broader publics provides cause for concern.[4]

I believe that in such a climate the theological conversation requires new methodological proposals that should seek to satisfy three principal criteria. First, they must offer the prospect of sufficient common ground to engage a variety of minds in the type of spirited reflection and debate that define a field of inquiry. But second, consensus must not be bought at the price of silencing or homogenizing different points of view, some of which have only recently been admitted to the discussion. Any proposed methodology must therefore possess sufficient flexibility to become an instrument for the expression of a variety of voices speaking on their own terms. And third, at a time of considerable cultural crisis and redefinition, new definitions of the theological task should seek to bridge the growing gap between the academy and society at large.

By considering the broad stream of the Christian tradition I represent, I am led to restate these criteria as follows. It seems that Christian discourse has survived and thrived when it displayed identity, catholicity, and relevance. By identity I mean that capacity, in spite of tensions and conflicts, to recognize a common set of texts, traditions, and practices that formed the common reference points for debate and inquiry. Under the rubric of apostolicity, Christian identity was usually understood diachronically as continuity with the witnesses who had gone before, but at any given moment the synchronic dimension of worldwide community was probably just as important.[5]

By referring to catholicity I wish to suggest that this community has always been characterized by internal tensions. From Paul's time onward Christianity found ways (never without great difficulty!) of incorporating spokespersons from vastly different cultures and social locations, and significant, ever-shifting local adaptations of the general discourse were the inevitable result. In the long run this flexibility permitted Christian discourse to maintain its basic coherence while becoming the cultural and intellectual property of many different peoples.[6]

The message of Christianity, centered on the narratives about Jesus, could find a home in so many settings precisely because it possessed the capacity to effectively address the genuine questions and concerns of persons. In times of great uncertainty and suffering representatives from all social classes, but probably those in the lower ranks in particular, heard a message of hope highly relevant to their experience, giving meaning to their struggles.[7]

This book represents one attempt to make a methodological proposal consonant with three criteria whose validity is acknowledged by a broad range of theologians. I do not pretend to present the best, let alone the only, valid way of conceiving of the theological task at the end of the twentieth century. As I will argue, however, theology conceived as the practice of rhetorical hermeneutics does represent a rather common way in which important premodern Christian thinkers pursued their intellectual labor. This approach calls attention to the shared textual basis of much past and present theological reflection, but by requiring various interpretations in ever new circumstances, it encourages the pursuit of catholicity and relevance as well. I will also suggest (nondogmatically, I hope) that as a form of argument and communication, no theologian can avoid involvement with the persuasive elements known as rhetoric.

My argument will unfold in the following sequence. Given the general unfamiliarity of theological students with the rhetorical tradition, the first chapter seeks to offer an introduction to the oratorical legacy of the West, with reference to its impact on the development of theology and hermeneutics. With this necessary background, the second chapter uses a common rhetorical device, namely, comparison and contrast with other scholars, to present the method of theology conceived as rhetorical hermeneutics. Since many modern persons equate rhetoric with sophistry, the third chapter offers some epistemological defense of the rhetorical ways of interpreting texts. And in the fourth chapter I seek to provide an example of the operation of this method by proposing rhetorical approaches to classical Christian doctrines of sin.

The ideas presented have developed in conversation with persons too numerous to mention here, but I should express my debt to two experts in theological rhetoric, William Bouwsma and David Cunningham. My colleagues at the Church Divinity School of the Pacific and the Graduate Theological Union would not let this project die when I was tempted to give it up. And above all I thank my mentor, Rebecca Chopp, for inspiring and guiding my rhetorical inquiry from the beginning, for offering unceasing encouragement, and for providing expert and elegant examples of persuasive interpretation and practice. I have learned the truth of the maxim that all scholarship is collaborative, regardless of the name that ends up on the title page. This study seeks to make some small contribution to the furtherance of a lively conversation about the future of theological work as we approach a new millennium.

CHAPTER ONE

An Introduction to the Rhetorical Tradition

Most students of theology have at least some familiarity with hermeneutics, but few are conversant with the Western tradition of rhetoric, an important part of the cultural legacy of Greece and Rome. For reasons pondered more fully below, the study and teaching of the oratorical art declined at the onset of the modern era. Trained in universities following the new scientific paradigms, most theologians therefore did not learn to recognize rhetorical devices at work in religious texts or to be very self-conscious about their own use of persuasive means. This chapter therefore seeks to provide a general orientation to the *ars rhetorica* that developed in antiquity and became a significant part of its legacy to Christian Europe.

Is Aristotle the Authority on Rhetoric?

While I employ a number of the now standard introductions to classical rhetoric, I differ from them and from their theological followers in one important respect. I choose to concentrate not on Greek but on Roman oratorical treatises. Cicero and Quintilian and not Plato and Aristotle guide my discussion. The continuing vitality of Plato's philosophy was a major factor in shaping the modern disdain for rhetoric. In the dialogue *Gorgias* the Athenian polemicized against the teachers of oratory, calling their art a "knack" comparable to cooking, "which aims at pleasure without consideration of what is best."[1] Even in his subsequent dialogue about true rhetoric, the *Phaedrus*, Plato's strict subordination of skillful speech to the control of philosophy, the proper discoverer of the true, betrays his deep suspicion of a practice he equates with sophistry.[2]

Given such hostile presuppositions, recent retrievers of the art of oratory have been forced to display persuasive astuteness. When Chaim Perelman and Lucy Olbrechts-Tyteca published their influential study, *The New Rhetoric: A Treatise on Argumentation*,[3] they chose the scientifically respectable Aristotle as their classical guide. In this choice they have been followed by most major writers on rhetoric, as well as by their theological appropriators. Thus David Tracy, who more than anyone pioneered theology's renewed attention to the arts of persuasion, writes: "The classic work [on rhetoric] remains Aristotle's."[4] He demonstrates no familiarity with Roman oratory. Similarly, in his award-winning work, *Faithful Persuasion: In Aid of a Rhetoric of Christian Theology*,[5] David S. Cunningham bases his discussion on Aristotle's *Rhetoric*, making only passing and mostly critical remarks about Cicero and Quintilian.

While I understand the argumentative context that made concentration on Aristotle preferable, as we move into the second generation of the rhetorical revival and in particular seek to reap its harvest for contemporary theology, I have strong reasons for taking a different (Roman) path. In the first place, in my desire to adhere to the criterion of identity or continuity, I must take cognizance of the fact that the Roman treatises decisively shaped the tradition of Christian eloquence in the West. However much prestige the philosophies of Plato and Aristotle may have enjoyed in other respects, their treatments of persuasiveness exerted little direct influence until the end of the twentieth century. As I will show, many of Aristotle's important technical contributions were communicated indirectly via his Roman successors. But the *Rhetoric* itself was virtually unavailable until the Renaissance — and even then it received second billing to newly published works by Cicero and Quintilian.[6]

Moving beyond historical considerations to constructive matters, I find that the Greek treatises offer a lukewarm endorsement of the rhetorical program. I wonder, then, if they can sustain a genuine recovery of oratorical method. I have already referred to Plato's deep suspicion. But on closer examination Aristotle isn't much of an improvement. Cicero, who repeatedly expressed his admiration for his great predecessor and makes ample use of his textbook, nonetheless perceptively observed that the master "thought [rhetoric] beneath him." The Roman knew the tradition according to which Aristotle would have avoided the subject had not his scholarly rivalry with Isocrates induced him to also devote his usual thoroughness to the latter's special competence, "practice in speaking."[7]

Little wonder, then, that the *Rhetoric* contains unmistakable hints of its author's ambivalence about its subject. In the first chapter Aristotle denounces the vital oratorical strategy of appealing to a judge's emotions, but he devotes much of the second book to cataloguing the ways in which speakers can sway passions.[8] In line with his consistent elitism, other passages suggest that Aristotle views rhetoric as a condescension to general human inability to sustain the rigor of rationality. He declares that "to contend by means of the facts themselves is just, with the result that everything except demonstration is incidental; but nevertheless, [delivery] has great power ... because of the corruption of the audience" (3.1.404a, pp. 218–19).[9]

My conviction that Aristotle "lacked a proper respect for the subject"[10] finds further corroboration when he suggests that classifying and defining are "not a matter for the rhetorical art but for a more profound and true [discipline]." After implicitly criticizing Isocrates for improperly enlarging the scope of oratory, Aristotle suggests that this art is a kind of half-breed midway between dialectic and "sophistic discourses." He concludes by drawing a distinction between "forms of knowledge of certain underlying facts" and rhetoric, which has knowledge "only of speech" (1.4.359b, p. 53). As we shall see, neither the Roman orators, their Christian students, nor many modern Aristotelian proponents of rhetoric find this dichotomy or its implied denigration of their art acceptable.[11]

I shall rely primarily on the treatises of Marcus Tullius Cicero (106–43 B.C.E.), then, to present a synopsis of the persuasive art. At those points where Marcus Fabius Quintilian (40–95 C.E.) goes beyond his master I will include his remarks as well.

The Tradition of Roman Oratory

In his first treatise, *De Inventione*, Cicero defined rhetoric in these terms: "we will classify oratorical ability as a part of political science. The function of eloquence seems to be to speak in a manner suited to persuade an audience, the end is to persuade by speech."[12]

In *De Oratore* Cicero insists that to perform this task the rhetor should acquire knowledge in virtually all subjects, for he considers "eloquence to be the offspring of the accomplishments of the most learned men [sic]" (1.2, p. 7). Cicero refuses to accept disciplinary specializations such as the separation of philosophy and rhetoric (3.16, pp. 208–9).[13] Faced with the charge, repeated often over the centuries, that in this way one sets an impossibly high standard for potential speakers, he insists in *De Oratore* that though he is presenting an ideal rhetor, "such a one as perhaps has never existed," sound pedagogy requires instilling a striving after the highest exemplar so that all will achieve the best skill within their ability.[14]

Cicero's exalted view of the province of the orator has at least two important consequences. First, it means that rhetoric will eventually become nothing less than a full-blown educational theory aimed at equipping and forming youths for responsible citizenship — what the Germans would later call *Bildung*.[15] Quintilian's *Institutio Oratoria* ("Education of the Orator") would be the unrivaled classic in this area for at least fifteen centuries.[16] The curriculum laid out for prospective speakers was formidable: civil law, history, literature, all areas of philosophy, the sciences, and the principles of rhetoric, accompanied by frequent practice in declamation.[17] Nothing that might assist the achievement of persuasion could be neglected, and every human endeavor would benefit from the grace supplied by rhetorical expression. For in the life of study eloquence reigns, as the humanist Lorenzo Valla later declared, as "queen of all things."[18]

The second consequence of Cicero's vision consists in the way in which he viewed eloquence as the most useful virtue for the maintenance of healthy human societies. His pedagogical recommendations in part aimed to counter Plato's charge that oratory could easily be misused toward ignoble ends, for Cicero insisted in *De Inventione* that the study of philosophical ethics and moral conduct, "which is the highest and most honourable of pursuits," would keep his vocation from being "harmful" (1.1, p. 5). Wisdom and eloquence must walk hand in hand, for "wisdom without eloquence does too little for the good of states, but ... eloquence without wisdom is generally highly disadvantageous and never helpful" (1.1, p. 3). Cicero speculates that a wise person's discovery of the principles of persuasion transformed the animal-like, violent condition of primitive humanity into peaceful social existence. While reason determined the necessary antecedents of political science, without eloquence people would never have been persuaded to voluntarily adopt the arrangements of civil life (1.2, p. 7).

If oratory thereby receives credit for laying the foundations of social concord, its continual cultivation also "renders life safe ...and even agreeable." Through activity in the law courts and legislative debates the rhetor prevents evil persons from inflicting private or public harm on the citizenry. Provided that it be ever accompanied by wisdom, eloquence will bestow innumerable benefits on every state (1.4, p. 13). What could therefore be more disastrous for the commonwealth than to neglect this art because some have abused it, or to separate its cultivation from the pursuit of philosophy?

Following this same line of reasoning, Quintilian defines the orator as "a good man [sic] skilled in speaking" — and he stresses that the former modifier exceeds the latter in importance.[19] In fact, he then proceeds to construct various arguments designed to prove that only virtuous persons can be truly persuasive. This constitutes the Roman version of Aristotle's ethical argument, the fact that the character of the speaker significantly affects the audience's willingness to be won over.

Having established the glorious nature and necessity of rhetoric, the Roman orators then detail how one might achieve the end of their noble vocation: persuasion.[20] Following Aristotle, they recognize three types of suasory speech, depending on the general cause involved. In law courts speakers utilize forensic or judicial rhetoric, which aims to establish guilt or innocence by reference to what has already occurred. In the assemblies of the people debaters employ deliberative oratory, which argues for the expediency of potential future courses of action. And on numerous occasions, including aspects of the former scenarios, eloquence expresses itself in the epideictic or demonstrative genre designed to please hearers in the present by praising or blaming individuals or qualities.[21]

But able persuaders will go beyond this rough division to follow the cardinal principle of their art, decorum, exalted by Cicero
in *De Oratore*. He defines the rhetor's lodestar in these terms:

> The eloquence of orators has always been controlled by the
> good sense of the audience, since all who desire to win ap-
> proval have regard to the goodwill of their auditors, and
> shape and adapt themselves completely according to this and
> to their opinion and approval. (8.24, p. 323)

The task of rhetoric, therefore, always remains essentially the
same: "to determine what is appropriate" and to "consider pro-
priety" (21.70, pp. 357–59). This will depend on the nature of the
subject and on the character of both the speaker and the listeners. Only the wise can perform the necessary and most difficult
act of discernment, so that once again virtue and eloquence are
intimately wedded in Cicero's rhetorical vision.[22] Without the
guiding hand of decorum none of the tasks enumerated next has
any prospect for success.

The Roman theorists discussed five stages involved in the production of a speech. First, one had to determine what content
to include through a process known as *invention*.[23] To facilitate
this task teachers developed two types of checklists. The first cata-
logued all conceivable causes that might be at issue, and the second
brought together a stockpile of arguments, examples, and maxims
appropriate to each, known as commonplaces (Greek *topoi*, Latin
loci). These inventories, which make such tedious reading for modern students, offered orators who memorized them a storehouse
from which judicious selections could be made according to the
requirements of decorum.

This material, once settled upon, then required the most effective possible arrangement through a procedure named *disposition*.
While the speech should be so constructed as to strike the
audience as a seamless whole, textbooks such as *De Oratore* recommended an invariable sequence of five distinct parts all oratorical
performances ought to contain (2.76–81, pp. 174–81). Speakers
should begin with an opening called the *exordium*, a kind of preface in which the listeners receive an introduction to the case the
orator will make and inducements to adopt a frame of mind recep-

tive to the argument. Next follows a brief, clear, and dispassionate statement of the basic facts and issues, the *narration*. In order to "weaken your adversary's supports, and strengthen your own" (2.81, p. 180) two closely related sections, the *confirmation* and the *refutation*, bring forth all the relevant evidence and varied commonplaces in favor of the orator's position before arranging material that attacks the soundness of the opposite point of view. The oration closes with a *peroration*, which emotionally incites the assembly or judge to render a favorable decision.

Having determined the basic structure and content of the presentation, orators next embarked on what they considered the essence of eloquence, the art known as embellishment or *elocution*. Here the power of words finds full expression. The concerns that make up this stage, then, are anything but merely stylistic, for the ability to persuade, in the view of *De Oratore*, depended precisely on the verbal forms in which ideas were cast. To imagine that thoughts could be judged apart from their expression struck Cicero as absurd.

Once again guided by the law of accommodation, the rhetor must first consider three general styles that correspond to three fundamental duties of the orator. The so-called low style is the most subdued, avoiding flourishes and relying on its "intellectual appeal," the instrinsic merit of the case (6.21, p. 319). Here the persuader carries out the responsibility of instructing the audience. The middle style mixes rational and emotional suasion in a pleasing fashion, thus discharging the obligation to delight. Finally, the grandiloquent style pulls out all the stops of passion as it moves the hearers. In Cicero's mind every effective discourse had to avail itself of this grand style to some degree, for "to sway is victory" (21.69, p. 357). Without moving the emotions of the audience the orator cannot achieve persuasion.

Evidently while in certain circumstances the nature of the case and the tastes of the audience would require the prevalence of one style, the various parts of a speech already outlined called for the use of each at particular points. The narration, for instance, clearly demands employment of the low style, while the grand style meets the requirements of the peroration. Within these broad parameters each orator receives encouragement to develop an individual style (*De Oratore* 3.7, p. 200). However, all should strive for elocution characterized by "pure Latin, with perspicuity, with gracefulness, and with aptitude and congruity to the subject in question" (3.10, p. 202).

After laying down these general principles Cicero turns to the building blocks of a good style. Since words constitute the compositional units, he treats their use first singly, then in combination. In consideration of the hearers the orator should use common words with a pleasing sound unless a point can be made more strikingly and economically by using an archaic term, a neologism, or a metaphor (3.38, pp. 235–36).

The analysis of the varieties of tropes leads to lengthy treatments of the figures or ornaments. These devices perform far more than a decorative function. The ancients believed that they permitted a skilled speaker to effectively externalize inner emotions and thoughts. Moreover, the figures served as weapons or instruments that did the work of persuasion. As Kenneth Burke aptly summarizes their appeal, "yielding to the form prepares for assent to the matter identified with it" (58).[24]

Cicero divides the figures into two types, those of thoughts and those of words. In the former category he includes examples such as digression, repetition, exaggeration, interrogation (the proverbial rhetorical question), the introduction of fictitious characters, and anticipation. Among the verbal ornaments he lists reiteration, variation, forcible emphasis, the stringing together of words with similar cadences or endings, gradation, puns, and enumeration (3.53–54, pp. 252–54).[25]

To ascertain the complete catching up of the auditors in the aesthetic experience of speech Cicero also devotes a considerable portion of *De Oratore* to rules about rhythm and assonance (3.44–50, pp. 242–50). While the specifics of this instruction are almost incomprehensible to modern readers, the psychological reality that the Romans recognized is familiar to us: namely, that a pleasing presentation makes us more likely to accept an orator's pitch.

The final aspects of the orator's work, *memory* and the *delivery* itself — the praxis of rhetoric — need not detain us here, important as they are for successful oral performance.[26]

It may appear that the Romans depicted rhetoric in exclusively spoken terms. But the fact that they defended and taught their art in written texts should invalidate such a judgment. In *De Oratore* Cicero advises students to write as much as possible, for "*writing is said to be the best and most excellent modeler and teacher of oratory*" (1.33, p. 42, emphasis original). Quintilian, agreeing that in "writing are the roots, in writing the foundations of eloquence" (10.3.3, vol. 2, p. 284), composes a small treatise on the unique and concrete aspects of redaction (10.3–5.13, pp. 283–96).

Moreover, the place of textual interpretation in the work of persuasion was recognized by the Roman orators. What we would now call legal hermeneutics represents a constant theme in Cicero's *De Inventione*. In Quintilian we also observe the beginnings of a rhetorical literary criticism. In order to obtain "*supplies of matter and words*" (10.1.5, p. 247, emphasis original) prospective orators must read widely. He recognizes that arguments from antiquity can prove "weighty," since persons generally presume that their promoters were free of "prejudice and partiality" (10.1.34, p. 254). At the beginning of his tenth book Quintilian offers a lengthy list of recommended poets, historians, philosophers, and speeches from which one can derive profit. While in listening we can get carried away, reading permits us to exercise better judgment as we peruse passages repeatedly. Quintilian calls for close, careful reading, noting both the overall structure and the composition of individual units. And while students should not presume to condemn their superiors, neither should they assume "that everything that great authors have said is necessarily perfect" (10.1.24, p. 252). His comments on the Greek and Roman works on his list exemplify a criticism both of content (he deplores obscenity, frivolity, superficiality) and of style, measured by the orator's standards, decorum being the principal criterion.

The Rhetorical Ethos

By way of summary it might be useful to review seven characteristics of Roman oratory that help account for the character of Christian rhetorical theology in premodern times and begin to suggest the continuing fruitfulness of rhetoric in our own era.

1. Rhetoric's scope is practical. Its practitioners share a concern for the safety and health of the commonwealth. Hence we have seen that Cicero refers to his art as a branch of political science. Rhetoric is an applied science, involved in litigation and public policy matters of every sort.

2. Rhetoric possesses a popular or public nature. The orator must appeal to the masses and so cannot afford to resort to arcane ideas or language. Thus while Cicero in many respects admired the Stoic philosophers, he chastises them for having "a manner of speaking which is...dry, strange, unsuited to the ear of the populace, obscure, barren, jejune, and altogether of that species which a speaker cannot use to a multitude" (*De Oratore* 3.18, p. 210). Oratory and discursive elitism are incompatible.

3. Rhetoric is active. Whether it is displayed in the courtroom or the Senate, oratory comprises a form of praxis, a way of effecting desirable private and public consequences. The Romans recognized that in many social situations words are deeds.

4. Effective rhetoric must be contextual. The principle of decorum demands constant adjustment to ever-changing audiences and causes. Perhaps for this reason the mature Cicero, writing in *De Oratore*, disdains textbook approaches, for he knows that at best he can instill a way of thinking that must find its own way in each concrete circumstance.

5. Rhetorical logic must display a contingent character. In part the previous point already signals this fact. But deliberative oratory in particular, with its emphasis on the future, reveals that in human affairs decisions must usually be made before all the facts are in, in an inescapable and perpetual state of imperfect knowledge. Rhetoric offers a technique by which persons can argue their way toward mutually agreed upon courses of action based on probability, not certainty, and "informed opinion," not "scientific demonstration."[27]

6. Rhetoric is polemical, or what Burke calls "agonistic" (52). Cicero frequently compares the training of the orator with that of the gladiator. He is acutely aware of dangers threatening individuals and the state as a whole and urgently insists that wise rhetors must join the fray if the right is to prevail.[28] The emphasis on the stirring of passion adds to the inherently combative tenor of

the persuasive profession. Philosophers may enjoy the luxury of quiet retreat in the search for truth, but Cicero warmly affirms that "it is the part of a wise man [sic] to concern himself with public affairs," with all their clamor and divisiveness (*De Oratore* 3.17, p. 210).

7. Finally, rhetoric exemplifies a holistic spirit in at least two respects. First, I noted Cicero's refusal to endorse narrow academic specialization. Second, the orator knows that human beings are complex, possessing affective as well as intellectual natures. Eloquence appeals to the whole person in rational, emotional, aesthetic, ethical, and volitional terms. The Romans readily accept this reality instead of resigning themselves to it with a sigh as Aristotle seemingly does.

The Appropriation of Rhetoric by Christian Theologians

In the West the authority of St. Augustine (354–430 C.E.) assured that the Roman rhetorical ethos would acquire a long-lasting Christian cast. His *On Christian Doctrine* exercised considerable influence, and it is a Ciceronian work. The saint never mentions or quotes Aristotle, but he includes citations from *De Inventione* and *De Oratore*.[29] The pedagogical purpose of Augustine's text becomes evident in the first line: "There are certain precepts for treating the Scriptures which I think may not inconveniently be transmitted to students" (3). Cicero's emphasis on the centrality of hermeneutics in legal practice is thus transferred to the Christian vocation of preaching and teaching. Augustine devotes most of his treatise to what we would now call rhetorical hermeneutics. In books 2 and 3 he demonstrates the ways in which the various biblical authors persuade through use of the three styles and recommends particular attention to the tropes and figures. These enable the now oft-criticized allegorical method, but that is not the only use Augustine makes of them. Attention to the way scriptural rhetors adapt themselves to their circumstances permits the historical interpretation favored in our age as well.

Book 1, in which Augustine presents his basic theory of symbols, also forms habits essential to proper use of sacred texts. This segment of the work represents a summation of Christian doctrine. It is therefore an example of the *loci communes*, those storehouses of quotes and basic arguments that served as a partially memorized reference source for practicing orators. Interpretative procedures and commonplaces together funded *inventio*, described above as the first stage of rhetorical composition, which Augustine describes as "a way of discovering those things which are to be understood" (7).[30]

The *telos* undergirding Augustine's book becomes manifest in the fourth book, a Ciceronian rhetorical treatise for preachers. Like the great Roman, Augustine refuses to write a book of rules, thus adhering to the fundamental principle of decorum. He acknowledges that oratory has been employed for noble and evil purposes but concludes that since "the faculty of eloquence, which is of great value in urging either evil or justice, is in itself indifferent, why should it not be obtained for the uses of the good in the service of truth" (4.2.3, pp. 118–19)? Augustine follows Cicero in outlining the three duties of speakers and the three styles, and he furthers his own version of the union of wisdom and eloquence by insisting that preachers must become "proficient in the Holy Scriptures" (4.5.7, p. 122). He places particular emphasis on the ability of persuasiveness to induce persons to engage in proper actions and heartily endorses the emotional appeal of the grand style, the effect of which becomes apparent "sometimes even through tears, and finally through a change of their way of life" (4.24.53, p. 161). This ethical outcome defines the purpose and practice of the rhetorical enterprise and can be expected only when the whole person, consisting of feelings as well as intellect, has been moved by the speech of the Christian orator/preacher.

The social circumstances of the medieval era led to a diminishment of the full civic practice of rhetoric as promoted by Cicero and Augustine, but Renaissance scholars vigorously retrieved the rhetorical ethos I have summarized.[31] And through their influence the persuasive arts decisively shaped the theology of the Reformation on both sides of the emerging division of Christendom. In spite of his misgivings about the greatest Northern champion of rhetoric, Desiderius Erasmus, Martin Luther's pedagogical interests caused him to frequently declare his deep admiration for Quintilian.[32] Trained as a humanist, John Calvin was an expert rhetorician. Persuasive methods colored the character of his doctrine. For instance, he used the technical term *accommodare* (a verbal synonym for decorum) to describe God's revelatory actions in the economy of salvation.[33] Even in the midst of the modern decline of rhetoric, important Christian thinkers would continue to stand in this tradition. John Henry Newman, for instance, went beyond homiletical deployment to develop an extensive rhetorical epistemology as an understanding of the nature of faith.[34]

Contemporary efforts to retrieve rhetorical theology, then, do not represent yet another fad but instead strive to adhere to the criterion of identity. Efforts such as the present work, however, face the challenge of modernity as, among other things, a concerted assault on the oratorical tradition. This introduction to rhetoric must therefore conclude with a consideration of the checkered fate of the persuasive arts since the late sixteenth century.

The Decline of Rhetoric

The modern period would threaten both religion and rhetoric.[35] What happened? Changes in pedagogy played a leading role. The well-organized method of Petrus Ramus exercised a powerful attraction in academic circles. Ramus went beyond Aristotle in his suspicion of rhetoric, limiting its role to ornamentation. Content derived through allegedly more reliable procedures, especially dialectical reasoning, might be presented in more pleasing verbal forms through the help of rhetoric, but otherwise Ramus refused to grant this dangerous discipline any place in his grand system of knowledge.[36] And the embrace of objectivism in the new empiricist and realist philosophies furthered a deep suspicion of the perceived vagaries of oratory. In his intellectual autobiography at the outset of his influential *Discourse on Method*, for instance, René Descartes admits that he "once esteemed eloquence highly" but had come to conclude that the study of rhetoric was useless, because "[t]hose who reason most cogently, and work over their thoughts, to make them clear and intelligible, are always the most persuasive." Along with the traditions of scholars and nations, theology, and the philosophy preceding him, Descartes thus rejected rhetoric, since "nothing solid could have been built on so insecure a foundation."[37]

But for our purposes the changes in the nature of reading itself seem most decisive. Jane Tompkins, one of the proponents of rhetorical hermeneutics today, offers a useful summary of the fate of rhetorical literature in the new scientific age.[38] She argues for a fundamental discontinuity between the assumptions about language that informed ancient literary criticism and those that govern most current textual interpretation. The ancients, all trained in rhetoric, realized that words represent "a form of power, and the purpose of studying texts from the past is to acquire the skills that enable one to wield that power" (203). In short, this classical literary approach, which still reigned in the Renaissance and survived up to the advent of the Enlightenment, concerned itself with action and behavior, not meaning: "literature is thought of as existing primarily in order to produce results and not as an end in itself" (204). Thus Renaissance poetry promoted patronage and courtship, while Augustan bards deployed verse as a satirical weapon with deadly political effect. In such a context it made no sense to create a specialization quarantined in the university and christened literary theory. Instead aesthetic production played a vital role at the heart of social existence.

But Tompkins notes that the wide dissemination of the technology of printing meant that the relationship between authors and their audience became ever more attenuated and impersonal. For each reader can now scrutinize a literary production in privacy.[39] Consequently an interest in the "psychology of reading" (215) emerged at the tail end of the Enlightenment of the eighteenth century. Moreover, the dominant role exercised by the paradigm of physical science spurred the study of literature to make itself respectable by engendering its own science of aesthetics, with appropriate institutional expressions in university departments everywhere. This move to safeguard the status of literary experience, however, at the same time isolated it further from common life, since its highly technical treatises, unintelligible to the uninitiated, could not sell well in mass markets.

Making the best of this situation, various theorists in the last two centuries have exulted in the "universal" role played by litera-

ture, unsullied as it is by partisan squabbles and routine matters —
a tendency reinforced by the internationalization of scholarship
enabled by new means of the distribution of books and journals.
The praise of their art as "a repository of eternal values" (217) entails an elite status for those qualified to decipher its mysteries.[40]
If the meaning of a text has become obscure, surely highly trained
specialists are needed to uncover its hidden riches, interpretation
now being an end in itself.

The bite in Tompkins's argument comes when she contends
that recent critical moves of various sorts, with all their self-
declared radicality, perpetuate this unclassical comprehension of
the nature and function of language. Her specific target is reader-
response criticism, which claimed to revolutionize hermeneutics
by shifting attention away from the objective structure of the
text championed by New Critical formalism to the subjective
experience of reading. Moreover, these critics appeared to revive
rhetoric, since they sought to trace how the author used various
textual stratagems in order to elicit affective responses in readers.[41]
On Tompkins's reading, however, in reader-centered approaches
the goal of criticism remains the elucidation of meaning. It appears to me that one frequently finds an analysis of how the writer
teaches readers how to read, but rarely an account of the practical
purpose this pedagogy aims to effect. Learning how to read represents just another approach to language as a depository of veiled
significations. In Tompkins's indictment "this approach does not
so much ignore the question of social relevance as postpone it,
assuming that until the text is rightly understood it cannot be
evaluated" (205) so that "response will be understood as a way
of arriving at meaning, and not as a form of political and moral
behavior" (206).[42] Thus in spite of appearances such theories of
reading have little to do with the ethos of classical rhetoric.

We may now observe abundant signs pointing to the revival
of rhetoric in religious studies. But do these retrievals represent a
recovery of the Roman ethos adopted by Augustinian and other
Western theologians? Or do they function as theological equiva-
lents of reader-response criticism? If so, what would a full-bodied
Ciceronian approach to theology as rhetorical hermeneutics look
like? I will seek to answer these questions in the next chapter.

CHAPTER TWO

Theology as Rhetorical Hermeneutics

There is increasing reason to believe that the reign of modernity approaches its end. The West has entered into a new era characterized by new norms of rationality. As is usual in times of transition, it will probably take some time to sort out the features of the emerging age of postmodernism.[1] Yet we may discern at least two clearly distinguishable characteristics. First, postmodern discourses seek in various ways to recover classical rhetoric. Friedrich Nietzsche, often considered the prophet initiating the break with modernity, based his philosophy on an analysis of the persuasive nature of language.[2] Second, scientism has received vigorous deconstructions. After Thomas Kuhn's groundbreaking book on *The Structure of Scientific Revolutions*, the method that decentered rhetoric as well as religion has been increasingly abandoned by practitioners of the physical and natural sciences. Rhetorical method increasingly spreads across the academic landscape, shaping discourses within and between disciplines formerly immune to its inducements.[3]

Given theology's penchant for adaptation to contemporary intellectual currents, such shifts have obviously affected the various disciplines pursued by faculty of seminaries and religion departments. Biblical scholars have led the way, producing an avalanche of studies pursuing the rhetorical criticism of the Hebrew Bible and the New Testament.[4] Students of homiletics have naturally continued to demonstrate interest in persuasive theory and methods.[5] Historical inquiry has moved beyond concentration on the rhetoric of individual Christian writers to ponder the ways in

---

I initially developed many of the ideas in this chapter in "Theology Update: The Incomplete Recovery of Rhetorical Theology," *Dialog* 34 (summer 1995): 187–92.

which even basic categories such as orthodoxy and heresy may represent persuasive constructions.[6] Now systematic theologians seem to have begun to catch up as well.

Contemporary Theology and the Rhetorical Ethos

Since the Enlightenment Western theology has had to face the fact of the increasingly marginal status of religion in modern society. In various ways, then, the practitioners of the discipline of systematic theology in the North Atlantic world have devised strategies designed to once more obtain a hearing in the increasingly secularized realms of the academy and society at large. Hermeneutical theory has been one technique employed by theologians to effect "publicness."[7] And while it seems somewhat exaggerated to claim that "in contemporary theology rhetoric has become a highly fashionable concept,"[8] I do detect a warming up to the seven characteristics of the rhetorical ethos (see chapter 1), as the following review should indicate.

1. *Method as practical and political.* Karl Barth declared that he wrote his massive dogmatics for preachers and that theologians should do their work with the Bible in one hand and today's newspaper in the other. Nor should we forget his spirited opposition to Nazism.[9] Guided by such examples, the fundamental practical and even political nature of theology has found diverse expressions in newer works by writers such as Johann B. Metz and Don Browning.[10]

2. *Public method.* Eschewing the opprobrium often attached to popularizers, a number of recent theologians have found ways to write in language that persons in the pew and street can understand without necessarily oversimplifying issues or losing profundity.[11]

3. *Method as praxis.* Latin American liberation theologians have stressed the primacy of praxis, though the insistence of some that theology as such constitutes a secondary moment of reflection upon previous engagement may obscure the way in which the discipline can in and of itself function as a praxis.[12] From the vantage point of a different theoretical paradigm George Lindbeck has also insisted on the active nature of religious discourse by de-

scribing the way in which the Christian "language game" shapes its adherent's response to the world.[13]

4. The contextuality of method. The growing multicultural realities of contemporary Christianity, together with the post-Enlightenment awareness of our historical and cultural situatedness, has brought a strong emphasis on contextuality in its wake in works by theologians such as Robert Schreiter and Aylward Shorter.[14]

5. Contingent method. The recent influence of postmodernism on theology has elevated an antifoundationalist epistemology.[15] But the view of human knowledge promoted by the ancient rhetoricians can be found in more classical sources. This would help account for the intense recent interest in Søren Kierkegaard's writings.[16]

6. Method as polemic. José Míguez Bonino, James Cone, and Elisabeth Schüssler Fiorenza exemplify the way in which writers representing groups struggling against oppression have insisted that theology inevitably takes sides, so that a polemical stance cannot be avoided.[17]

7. Wholistic method. In his frequently quoted writings on theological education Edward Farley laments the separation of theology as sapiential knowledge from its form as an academic discipline and opposes the loss of a united pedagogical vision amid the fragmented pursuit of specializations in universities and seminaries.[18] And no one has stressed the unity of the affective and intellectual dimensions of human existence more than did the founder of modern dogmatics, Friedrich Schleiermacher. After an eclipse under the concerted attack of neo-orthodoxy Schleiermacher's influence appears to be shining brightly once more.[19]

As I suggested at the outset, then, theo-logos as discourse will inevitably become a rhetorical performance. But in spite of this commonality of interest between contemporary theology and oratory, few systematicians appeal to the resources provided by the traditions of persuasive art.[20] Moreover, I must ask whether those who do so, in spite of the best of intentions, can escape the force of the indictment of Jane Tompkins and Steven Mailloux.

Rhetorical Theology and Philosophical Hermeneutics: David Tracy and His School

In the United States David Tracy's Roman Catholic hermeneutical theology has been one of the more influential proposals for the renewal of theology's public role. Focusing on the notion of a classic, which would by definition not obtain its status unless it enjoyed widespread public appeal, Tracy declares that the "systematic theologian is nothing more nor less than the interpreter of the religious classics of a culture."[21] He admits that his works have sought to provide an intellectual defense of the Christian faith, at least to the extent of protesting against the neglect of religious texts, for they represent that special genre that addresses inescapable questions of ultimate meaning.[22]

Hermeneutical theologies must inevitably rely on some relation to rhetoric, the ancient art of persuasion. In *Plurality and Ambiguity* Tracy suggests that "modern hermeneutical discourse analysis...is, after all, only a modern return to, and rethinking of, both ancient rhetoric and earlier hermeneutics" (65). Another comment reveals how in Tracy's view rhetoric constitutes one of several significant modes of investigation: "In any inquiry, argument is often needed. Even modern poetics needs dialectics and rhetoric....Dialectics and rhetoric, in turn, need ethics and politics at some point to complete the larger inquiry" (24).

It would be manifestly unfair to attach all of the unflattering characterizations of modern hermeneutics sketched by Tompkins to Tracy's scholarship. And in the limited space available here I can hardly do justice to the fullness of his significant theological contribution. I should note that he explicitly rejects elitism, and with regard to political options he recognizes that "not to choose is itself a choice."[23] Specifically, he does not consider the massive suffering of the innocents "one subject among many" but validates the preferential option for the poor thematized by liberation theologians.[24]

And yet Tompkins helps me to see that on the whole Tracy's work is guided by an understanding of language that centers on meaning and sees misunderstanding and not suffering as the primary problem demanding a solution. Put differently, I would conclude that Tracy specializes in the type of inquiry pursued in books 1–3 of Augustine's *On Christian Doctrine*, while thus far he has scarcely addressed the concerns of book 4. And it seems to me that Ciceronian rhetoric — which, to use one of Tracy's felicitous phrases, I am "retrieving" — had a different conception of language that aimed not at understanding but at action.[25]

While *Plurality and Ambiguity* clearly indicates that he did not intend it to be so, Tracy's order of priority can have the effect of decentering the conception of theology as a discourse that exercises discursive power in civil society. And there are good reasons for believing that even unawares and unintentionally our discipline always exerts such influence for good or ill, in support of re-formation or the status quo. While no one can foresee and thus forestall all such unanticipated consequences, I believe Tracy would agree with Míguez Bonino when he says that "we [must] face the responsibility for the concrete historical performative significance of our theological discourse."[26]

To summarize, my purpose has not been to invalidate Tracy's hermeneutical approach, from which I have derived considerable benefit. Indeed, Tracy's seminal role in promoting rhetorical theology must be acknowledged. Students of his such as Walter Jost and Stephen Webb have made significant contributions to the recovery of persuasive method. Jost drew constructive suggestions from his interesting study of Newman's rhetoric and is editing important volumes of collected essays on rhetoric.[27] Webb has concentrated on the rhetorical figure of hyperbole (reinscribed as the postmodern category of excess), offering creative interpretations of diverse authors (John Calvin, Barth, Georges Bataille, Flannery O'Connor) as well as a constructive proposal regarding the triune God.[28] True to their mentor, thus far both have concentrated on the use of rhetoric as an interpretative tool and as a way of opening up space for genuine plurality.[29] Webb's self-critique, however, demonstrates the potential of this approach to arrive at a more complete retrieval of Roman oratory. He writes:

> Although in [previous work] some substantive theological reflections emerged from my interest in rhetoric, once I achieved some distance from them I became dissatisfied with

their limited focus. It is too easy, as many postmodernists demonstrate, to brandish the category of excess without reflecting on the problems of social structure and moral duty.... By focusing on the phenomenon of gift giving, I have tried to find a place where excess and ethics intersect.[30]

As a second-generation member of this school (having been mentored by Tracy's student Rebecca Chopp), in this work I seek to learn from my elders by pointing to the intersection of theological rhetoric and moral action.

Faithful Persuasion: The Contribution of David Cunningham

Those interested in the recovery of rhetorical theology surely found encouragement when David S. Cunningham's *Faithful Persuasion: In Aid of a Rhetoric of Christian Theology* won the Bross Prize in 1990. This author makes much more extensive and explicit use of rhetorical tools than Tracy's work does. Cunningham displays an impressive familiarity with contemporary communicative theory. As stated in his introduction, he aims to "suggest that Christian theology is best understood as *persuasive argument*" (5, emphasis original) and believes that a "rhetorical approach... can shed light on the process of argumentation" (7) characteristic of systematics.

Like the Tracy school, Cunningham considers Aristotle's work definitive, so he organizes his book around the three forms of persuasion, *pathos, ethos,* and *logos.* In my judgment this work succeeds on its own terms, namely, as theological prologomena. It functions as an analysis of language, including the doctrinal variety, demonstrating that all discourses have inherent persuasive effects. Cunningham offers a critique of Tracy's approach quite similar to the one I developed in the previous section. By perhaps somewhat unfairly critiquing Tracy's "contemplative endeavor" (Cunningham, 64), he expresses his belief that theology always moves persons toward action as well as the grasping of meaning. And Cunningham therefore affirms the potential of rhetoric as a catechetical instrument of conversion by which persons may be fully persuaded to adopt the Christian faith and lifestyle (95–97). And yet I wonder if his work thus far represents much of an improvement on the efforts of Tracy and his students. I offer three critical questions to further critical discussion with my friend and rhetorical collaborator. First, does Cunningham's work move beyond the hermeneutical orbit to embrace the ethical concerns of Augustine's fourth book? Second, does he appreciate the wholistic nature of rhetorical anthropology, in particular its insistence that the emotions must be engaged if persons are to accept the demands of orthopraxis? And third, does he adhere to the criterion of identity by fully appreciating the varied resources of the Roman/Christian rhetorical traditions?

1. In his final chapter, when he analyzes the praxis of Christian theology in the light of rhetorical theory, Cunningham singles out the hermeneutical task of "writing rhetorical histories." As I do below, he invokes the work of the literary critic Mailloux to describe what this entails. Thus Cunningham states that "the historian should raise questions about…political commitments" (239) — a critical aspect of the literary practice Mailloux advocates. But when the former tries his hand at writing a rhetorical account of Luther's involvement in the eucharistic controversies the theme of the political drops out (240–52). Cunningham limits himself to discussing the usefulness of this interpretative approach for "the analysis of the concrete situation in which persuasive arguments are developed and deployed" (240) in textual artifacts, but he gives no account either of the embeddedness of Luther's discourse in larger political questions of the Reformation era or of the way the construction of such histories in and of itself becomes the rhetorical promotion of practical, political purposes in our day. *Faithful Persuasion* contains only the briefest references to practical applications (216–19 and 252–54, for instance). If in his major methodological statement Cunningham therefore does not move beyond the hermeneutical confines characteristic of Tracy and his school, in more recent work he too has paid increasing attention to the connection between rhetorical theology and the formation of ethical disposition.[31]

2. Cunningham's concentration on Aristotle's rhetorical theory leads him to share the philosopher's uneasiness with the

emotional appeal. He quickly shifts the emphasis of *pathos* to an analysis of the audience (42–51) in a way not even found in *On Rhetoric*. As I argued in the previous chapter, understanding the audience through the metacategory of *decorum* precedes the analysis of the different paths to persuasion and the corresponding processes of invention. By not giving the emotional appeal its due I believe Cunningham unintentionally undercuts the type of wholistic approach to human persons that is a fundamental characteristic of the rhetorical *ethos*.

3. Cunningham shows great admiration for Augustine's *On Christian Doctrine*, but by deprecating the contribution of Cicero and Quintilian he does not appreciate how much the tradition they represent formed the saint's persuasive theory and practice.[32] And unfortunately he passes over the Renaissance as a "brief revival of rhetoric" (19–20). A period of at least two hundred years is hardly episodic, and in any case the consequences of this rebirth were immense — quite possibly including the Protestant Reformation.[33]

I have suggested that one strength of a rhetorical method is that, by being subject to various uses by different agents in diverse social locations, it embodies the virtue of catholicity. My work naturally differs from that of Tracy's school and Cunningham's work in that, to use Tracy's term, I am aiming at a different public. Perhaps Tracy writes primarily for the academy, while Cunningham addresses the church. The latter uses rhetoric to reconceptualize theology as a catechetical and evangelizing activity. These activities certainly express key components of the church's mission. But the people of God are also called to *diakonia* on behalf of victims. A focus on the conversion of persons to Christianity does not necessarily entail the changes in behavior stressed so often by classical orators. As Cunningham would recognize, this different yet related duty involves addressing a different case to a different audience. To borrow an interesting distinction drawn by Jon Sobrino, when attempts have been made to stand with the oppressed "the adversary of theology hasn't been so much the 'atheist' as the 'non-man' [sic]."[34] In my effort to retrieve all aspects of Ciceronian/Augustinian rhetoric, I aim to address my work primarily to Tracy's third public, namely, society at large.

Lest I exaggerate the originality of my own contribution, however, I must discuss the contemporary rhetorical paradigm to which I owe the greatest debt.

The Power to Speak:
Rebecca Chopp's Rhetoric of Liberation

As I already mentioned, Chopp also studied with Tracy, but her interest in the theologies of liberation have consistently led her to a greater emphasis on the concerns of Augustine's fourth book. Her *The Power to Speak: Feminism, Language, God*[35] might at first blush appear to align with the works discussed above. As a student of Tracy, she too knows only Aristotle's classical work on persuasion. But appreciative comments about Augustine and Calvin indicate that something different is at work here (23, 65, 131). And she employs a number of critical linguistic and social theories that, as Tompkins emphasizes, have "come to occupy a position very similar to, if not the same as, that of the Greek rhetoricians for whom mastery of language meant mastery of the state," since they focus on "the relations of discourse and power" (226). Thus Chopp defines feminist theology as "discourses of emancipatory transformation that proclaim the Word to and for the world" (3).[36] In particular her book seeks to make a political contribution to the overcoming of gender oppression in church and society.[37]

One of Chopp's strategies involves the use of hermeneutics, illustrated by her interpretation of Luke 4:16–30 (40–70). But the decisive influence of Elisabeth Schüssler Fiorenza's work means that the category of the political is now located in the foreground.[38] This is the conception of the hermeneutical task embodied in this book. Chopp has acknowledged the importance of rhetoric in the textual work necessary to emancipatory praxis.[39] But she makes more frequent and extensive use of American pragmatic philosophy to pursue our common agenda.[40]

Following Chopp's lead, this work seeks to round out the recovery of rhetorical hermeneutics by making the connections between pre- and postmodern method even more explicit than she does. I suspect that much of the persuasive appeal of discourses of liberation in the United States will depend on the ability to demonstrate that this approach to theology is not novel but in more than superficial continuity with traditional practices of theological production.[41] Moreover, I perceive a need for additional and more extended examples of rhetorical hermeneutics at work. As rhetoricians have always known, specific illustrative cases have enormous persuasive power. Given the frequently mentioned pragmatic penchant of the "American mind,"[42] performances of the method will be necessary if systematic theologians in the United States are to be persuaded to accept this intellectual practice as a modus operandi. I will turn to that task in the final chapter, but first I would like to provide a comprehensive summary of my proposed method for pursuing theology as rhetorical hermeneutics.

Rhetorical Hermeneutics Today

I propose that while the case we wish to make may differ, the manner in which theologians make rhetorical use of texts in the task of invention is in essence the same as that followed by certain so-called secular literary critics. Moving beyond reader-response criticism, Tompkins and a number of her colleagues are attempting to return discussions of literature to the public marketplace of ideas. This approach admits that its study of texts is "interested." As Terry Eagleton writes, "rhetoric has always wanted to find out the most effective way of pleading, persuading and debating, and rhetoricians studied such devices in other people's language in order to use them more productively in their own" (206–7). Frank Lentricchia contends that "the point is not only to interpret texts, but in so interpreting them, change our society." He defines the test by which this textual procedure asks to be judged: "Does one's approach to the text enable or disenable — encourage or discourage — oneself and one's students and readers to spot, confront, and work against the political horrors of one's time?"[43]

But Mailloux has provided both the name for this method and the most complete account of its operation. In recognizing and establishing a practical dialogue between the rhetorical horizon of the interpreter and the rhetorical horizon of the text, rhetorical hermeneutics moves through the following steps.

First the interpreter must distinguish one's own interpretation from that others have given of the same subject. Readers are thus persuaded one more treatment of, say, theology and rhetoric merits their attention, since previous discussions are either inadequate or at least incomplete in certain respects. Mailloux calls this "embed[ding] the act of interpretation first in its most relevant critical debates" (134). I have attempted to model this procedure in the preceding sections.

But specific critical performances are always theory-laden. Therefore Mailloux realizes that "the act and its participation in ongoing arguments must be situated...within relevant institutional discourses" (134). In the previous chapter we saw how Tompkins performs this task. In his turn Mailloux distinguishes his approach from other critical methods such as the formalism of the New Criticism (19–53). I will offer a version of this task in the next chapter.

Furthermore, like all aspects of persuasive theory rhetorical hermeneutics must be ruled by the principle of decorum. Mailloux insists that "the interpretive act, its arguments, and its framing institutions must be placed within the cultural conversations, relevant social practices, and material circumstances of its historical moment" (134). Without attention to the wider setting of its intended audience, which must include the political landscape, no interpretive theory could realistically expect to gain acceptance. In particular, the interpreter must trace the way power relations are both represented and exercised through discursive means (136–41). Rhetorical hermeneutics, like the theology of liberation, assumes that there is no such thing as a politically neutral act of interpretation.[44]

Finally, the literary critic must reconstruct the audience addressed in a text, the issues at stake, and the views and actions of the opponents the writer seeks to refute. In other words, the textual artifact is read as a rhetorical performance with persuasive ends. Mailloux demonstrates this facet of his method by offering a lengthy interpretation of Mark Twain's *The Adventures of Huckleberry Finn* (57–129). In the final chapter I will read Augustine's and Calvin's statements on sin as a rhetorical theologian, which will require me to incarnate them as polemical thinkers in their time and place.

I might note that as just described the method of rhetorical hermeneutics seems to honor the theological criterion of identity through its serious engagement with the records of the Christian past (steps 1 and 4); that of catholicity through its recognition of historical particularities (steps 3 and 4); and that of relevance through its attention to contemporary debates and concerns (steps 2, 3, and 4).

In line with the second step of Mailloux's program, it seems wise to counter a key objection to a rhetorical course. The fifth characteristic of the persuasive ethos, contingent method, is probably the most controversial. Yet rhetorical hermeneutics can scarcely avoid it.

Any writer assumes that his or her readers could read between the lines; the author did not need to state all the presuppositions and implicit knowledge held in common with contemporary readers. But we enjoy only a limited communion with past authors, severely attenuated by the passage of time. Put differently, we possess texts but have access to contexts only through these and other written records. If we are to make any sense of written statements, then, I know of no way of avoiding the attribution of intentions. And since our predecessors are no longer available for an interview (though these often fail to resolve doubts), it is impossible to know with certainty whether or not a guess about motives corresponds to the persuasive aims held.

Reflecting on the debate about intentionality in recent literary theory, Stanley Fish notes that

> if it is by means of the intentional context and not directly that a reader imputes meaning to a text, that context must itself be imputed — given an interpreted form — since the evidence one might cite in specifying it — the evidence of words, marks, gestures — will only be evidence, have a certain shape rather than another, if its own shape has already (and interpretively) been assumed.[45]

In other words, proponents of rhetorical hermeneutics have no illusions about their ability to provide proof beyond all reasonable doubt. They set themselves the far more limited goal of persuasion and wager that conviction suffices.[46] And so the Ciceronian tradition of interpretation in which I locate myself avoids, or at least decenters, analytic and foundationalist method. The next chapter seeks to explain this choice, defend the epistemology that underlies it, and uncouple the linking of contingent logic with fideism and moral relativism.

CHAPTER THREE

Rhetorical Epistemology

Rhetorical hermeneutics rests upon the presupposition that discourses deployed to persuade persons to act in ways consonant with the public good can often do without the particular rigor characteristic of analytical reasoning. But since Plato's time many fear that appeals to emotions and other departures from the verities of math-like logic or empirical facticity must inevitably lapse into sophistry. In light of my purposes, I must take such critiques seriously, since they are sometimes voiced by the proponents of liberation theology.

The Brazilian theologian Clodovis Boff, for instance, writes that

> liberation theologians oppose what they call "theology of genitives," in which liberation would be no more than "one subject among many." Their claim, on the contrary, is that liberation is a kind of "horizon" against which the whole tradition of the faith is to be read. This methodological position, and its results, as I understand them, can, I think, yield only a *rhetoric*, not an *"analytic"*: discourse embroidered with many an "as to," instead of theory textured throughout with a single, powerful "in the light of."[1]

Since scholars with whom I feel considerable kinship worry that the abandonment of analytic approaches leads to moral relativism, I must establish that rhetoric does not draw or encourage this link. In fact, I contend that rhetoric does not even entail epistemological relativism. The first chapter suggested that it is absurd to charge the rhetorical theory of Cicero or Quintilian with immorality or disdain for truth and knowledge. The antirhetorical attempts made since Plato's time to promote a method untainted by sophistry are unnecessary and indeed harmful to the cause of truth, since they claim more than they can credibly demonstrate and thus tend to clear the path for that which they most fear, namely, skepticism.

In this chapter I will defend these theses in four stages. First I will fill out my description of rhetorical hermeneutics in order to suggest that this approach to texts rules out relativism from the start. Then I will compare and contrast my own position with the work of a liberationist author, Sharon Welch, who seems to argue in favor of relativism. Third, I will attempt to directly refute the claim that analytical method offers more reliable access to reality and hence to social efficacy. Fourth, I will suggest that the Christian doctrine of sin rules out the possibility of human knowledge more certain than that which persuasion may achieve. In summary, I argue that a viable theological method need embrace neither relativism nor objectivism.[2] As Rebecca Chopp suggests, a rhetorical approach aims to "stress the authority of theology as a product of persuasion in dialogue," where the standard of "warranted assertability" suffices.[3]

Rhetorical Hermeneutics Revisited

I have admitted that the rhetorical retrieval of texts must impute intentions and proffer conjectures about context. How then can I claim that this textual method avoids the kind of unsubstantiated assertions characteristic of sophistry? Doesn't my brand of hermeneutics require having what Plato called a knack for something not unlike the imprecision and guesswork of cookery? Won't any pleasing rendition of textual signification pass muster?

Two factors mitigate against this unfavorable verdict. In the first place, rhetorical hermeneutics insists that there definitely *is* a text in this class.[4] Steven Mailloux explains how his work is a reaction to the "idealistic" excesses of reader-response criticism (the text is what the reader makes it), which in turn rejected the "realistic" extremism of New Critical formalism (the structure of the text imposes one correct interpretation; 5–14). To illustrate: a rhetorical interpretation of John Calvin's *Institutes* would take the labors of those who have prepared critical editions of his Latin and French texts for granted and therefore assumes that certain words appear in Calvin's masterpiece in certain orders while others do not. My reading must make sense of these given terms, paragraphs, pages, and sections and of their sequence in the structure of the whole. I cannot make Calvin's text say whatever I think it should say. Few readers of the *Institutes* will lend any credence to my construal of the Reformer's purpose and argument unless my theory makes sense of this particular set of written data in its totality. In this respect the existence and content of the sheer physical text impose inescapable restraints on an interpreter's flights of fancy. "Textual positivism" cannot produce one incontestable answer to the riddle of Calvin's theology; rhetorical criticism also rejects structuralist hermeneutics. But careful attention to the linguistic units that were undeniably included in the final Latin and French versions of his compendium should circumscribe a range of acceptable variation. To use an extreme example, no one claiming to find a discussion of nuclear arms in the *Institutes* has much hope of persuading most conceivable audiences. *Contra* extreme reader-response criticism, then, the rhetorical use of texts does not involve creating them in one's own image. Textual artifacts represent an irreducible objective pole within the overall process of interpretation.[5]

In one sense the first point represents a particular instance of the second consideration, which holds that any assertions about textual meaning must be warrantable. The construal of signification must be defended; the rhetorical critic must offer a credible argument in support of specific hermeneutical inferences. Mailloux insists that "one does not...have to become a foundationalist theorist" when aiming to "disagree effectively" with other renditions (180). But he goes on to state that

> one simply and *rigourously* argues for a counterinterpretation, making such rhetorical moves as pointing to the text, citing the author's intentions, noting the traditional reading, and invoking the consensus.... The resulting interpretation is, of course, just as contingent...and could be just as open to further debate...[but] such historical contingency does not disenable interpretive argument, because it is truly the only ground it can have.... If no foundationalist theory will resolve disagreement over poems or treaties, *we must always*

argue our cases. In fact, that is all we can ever do. (180–81, emphasis added)

Several points in this quotation merit comment. First, I have already alluded to the first three argumentative moves Mailloux mentions ("pointing to the text," "citing the author's intentions," and taking cognizance of the "traditional reading" — or rather, the traditional readings). But his fourth strategy — "invoking the consensus" — has become particularly popular in recent epistemological debates. A number of writers[6] believe that the existence of social norms at any given point in history means that relativism is rarely if ever an option.

If this claim is read as an invocation of the principle of decorum I have no quarrel with it. Any successful rhetorician must recognize that audiences are loyal to well-established conventions, so that in any particular persuasive instance just anything will not do.[7] But Ciceronian orators aim precisely to use these cherished truths as means in a process by which listeners are moved to consider new realities. Since social constructionists readily admit that truths are being replaced by new ones all the time — their argument hinges on such radical historicity — I fail to see how their theory solves the problem of relativism. Their case involves a definition of relativism as individualistic subjectivism, but that represents only one aspect, albeit an important one, of the doubts raised by the antirhetorical forces. The defense of rhetoric hermeneutics will therefore require more than this.

My doubts about accepting the existence of "interpretive communities"[8] as a sufficient guarantee against nihilism have been reinforced by my studies of the Holocaust. The majority of the German people and their allies in places such as the Netherlands were united in their conviction that Jews represented a menace to European civilization. If truth is what the social order declares to be normative, on what basis can one argue that the genocide carried out by the Nazis was wrong? Is it enough to declare that different social traditions hold divergent ethical views? The very existence of antirhetorical forces throughout the ages[9] suggests that many persons find such reassurances rather less than persuasive.

I am therefore gratified that Mailloux does not place all his eggs in this fourth basket. But I believe that a reconsideration of the classical Roman orators could offer further argumentative resources and simultaneously deflect the Plato-like critiques of eloquence. Recall that Cicero and Quintilian recommended a rigorous education for prospective pleaders, an education that included many sciences but gave particular prominence to ethics. The complete formation of an orator, then, should produce persons committed to the never-ending quest for truth[10] and devoted to the common welfare. In the Christian context Augustine, Calvin, and others recommended thorough grounding in the Holy Scriptures and in both classical and contemporary sources addressing the issues of theology, spirituality, and polity. I am willing to wager that most persons spurred to extensive exposure to the Christian sources will perceive the centrality of what Albert Schweitzer called the "ethic of reverence for life."[11] Christian rhetors involved in the lifelong process of *Bildung* — simultaneously intellectual and spiritual — may, and indeed must, make numerous strategic adaptations, but the fundamental regulative principles, namely, love of God and love of neighbors, are nonnegotiable. If the worldview named relativism implies possible relativizing of the worth of concrete lives, Christians can have no share in it.[12]

The other matter I find intriguing in Mailloux's declaration involves his insistence on the omnipresent human need and duty to argue, and to argue rigorously. He and a number of other contemporary theorists eschew foundationalism's other guise, essentialism — and with good reason, as I will maintain below. And yet I perceive an implicit quasi-essentialism in the featured quote that is characteristic of antifoundationalist polemics generally.[13] It seems to promote an anthropology that construes our species as a collection of inherently argumentative creatures. Here the continuity with classical rhetorical sources is striking. Cicero and Quintilian always assumed that human beings can be persuaded, that skillful appeals to emotions, character, and reason will have the desired practical and active social effects. In fact, they believed that rhetorical figures corresponded to the given nature of the human mind.[14] As the consideration of Jane Tompkins's

article in chapter 2 suggested, they believed that human words exercise power. Therefore it always remained worthwhile to work
diligently at invention, disposition, and adornment of oral and
written weapons. The rhetorical worldview, then, does involve a
definite belief in realities that underlie and transcend particular social formations.[15] And by the same token, though Cicero wrote in
the tragic final days of the Republic and the bitter time of power
struggles characteristic of the early Empire, and Quintilian oper-
ated in the hostile context of imperial absolutism, the thought of
both is pervaded by an optimistic confidence that the truth will
prevail and that justice can be achieved. This hopeful character of
classical Roman oratory contrasts with some expressions of the
liberationist paradigm.

Nihilism and Liberation

A study like the present one must pay close attention to the work
of the feminist theologian of liberation Sharon D. Welch.[16] For her
contribution at first seems to be an instance of one of those modern theories that in Tompkins's view parallel the ancient rhetorical
viewpoints. In *Communities of Resistance and Solidarity* Welch
writes: "discourse has effects of truth... it does matter. Discourse
does, in some complex way, shape our world" (29). She labels her
genealogical method, derived from that of the French intellectual
historian Michel Foucault, as "strategic" and oriented "toward action" (55). Moreover, she takes the phenomena of human evil in
the twentieth century with radical seriousness, insisting that theology must be broken open by the profound challenge of massive
suffering (5–6). As I will, she recognizes the way in which all
human insights, including her own, are "tainted by sin, the power
of oppression" (86). Moreover, as the deep concern about nuclear
war thematized in *A Feminist Ethic of Risk* reveals, virtually every
page she has composed manifests her reverence for human lives.

And yet critical methodological differences distinguish my approach from hers. For Welch candidly confesses her lack of faith
in the possibility of persuasion. Speaking of the "nihilistic pole"
of her thought, she points to her "skepticism as a North American and my real fear that the human race might not be capable of

actual conversion to the other on anything but a socially insignificant, individual scale" (14). She questions the efficacy of human speech when she writes that to "denounce the arms race, for example, as unjust is *merely* a declarative act. It does not actually challenge that structure and may even function as a dangerous illusion that in the denunciation something has been accomplished" (82, emphasis added).[17] Further evidence for an antirhetorical attitude emerges in her discussion of conversation and dialogue, when Welch eschews "one-sided . . . 'dialogue' of persuasion of the other" as necessarily oppressive (87).[18]

The context of the latter quote reveals the central difference between Welch's contribution and my own. Like her, since I embrace the criterion of catholicity I am wary of a "too hasty imposition of commensuration" (87) but do not therefore adopt a communicative theory of radical incommensurability.[19] My presuppositions require me, in spite of an antifoundationalist epistemology, to formulate argumentative warrants seeking to persuade the unconvinced to commit themselves to the ethic of reverence for lives. I assume that human beings have the capacity to be moved by persuasive presentation of viewpoints external to their own experience, so that conversion to others remains an ever-present possibility. Welch's own journey (79) exemplifies how a white middle-class North American woman who, as she insists, possesses a double identity, oppressor and oppressed (ix), came to stand in solidarity with oppressed groups from vastly different social and confessional matrices. But her theoretical paradigm leads her to appeal to no warrant outside her own experience, so that she speaks of the "extreme contingency and probable arbitrariness of my own projects" (91). She readily admits that her critiques make sense solely on the basis of a prior commitment to the liberation of the oppressed which can itself have no rational basis (74–75). Welch's adherence to incommensurability, then, represents a kind of fideism. She can describe her own position, but defending it would in her view be an instance of the very ethic of control that she strenuously criticizes.[20]

The corollary of Welch's epistemological standpoint is a marked pessimism about the possibility of achieving justice in the United States (86).[21] She claims that "the fear that liberation may be either structurally or contingently impossible is internally required by liberation faith" (87). My respect for human lives, however, leads me to the opposite conclusion. I fear, first, that such notions may disenable the bracing hope required to challenge the status quo.[22] And second, I worry that giving up on the persuasive possibility opens the door to contemplation of the only other way by which oppressors can be made to stop their oppression, namely, physically eliminating them.[23] That unanticipated consequence would, I feel certain, displease Welch, and I therefore call for a reconsideration of the wisdom of promoting paradigms of incommensurability. Else we are seemingly left with two alternatives: the inevitable continuation of the status quo or violent revolution.

This process of rethinking might be furthered by applying the strategy of retrieval characteristic of rhetorical hermeneutics to the work of Welch's philosophical mentor, Michel Foucault.[24] In *A Feminist Ethic of Risk* she states her understanding of a preeminent aspect of the legacy he bequeathed to her: "I agree with him that it is possible to recognize the partiality of another system of logic and, I would add, of ethics, only when that system is no longer one's own" (4). Particularly during his early archaeological period of the 1960s,[25] Foucault depicted the power of ruling, yet historically contingent, epistemes (roughly akin to Max Weber's *Weltanschauungen*)[26] in determining what would count as true. One can thus readily conclude that he is recognizing the impossibility of escape from the restraints of worldviews made a very part of the constitution of subjects through the operation of disciplinary technologies always characterized by the intertwined effects of power/knowledge.[27] Welch's reading of his work, then, can base itself on numerous textual passages. If she is right, Foucault's authorship does not aim to persuade anyone but merely offers a historical description of the ongoing struggles between competing and equally plausible contingent truths.

But I contend that a rather different construal of Foucault's intent also possesses considerable textual support. James W. Bernauer has recently argued for the centrality of the metaphor of "force of flight" in Foucault's writings as a whole.[28] From this perspective the French genius was involved in a lifelong search for modes of analysis and intellectual praxis that would permit a break with patterns of thought that had driven the West along a forced march toward Auschwitz and Hiroshima and still hold us in their grasp. This schema of interpretation permits attention to Foucault's various methods — archaeological, genealogical, and so on — as shifting rhetorical strategies designed to undercut the allegiance his readers gave to intellectual systems possessing lethal consequences. I hope that by pointing to a few textual passages I might plant the possibility in readers' minds that Foucault may not be the complete relativist Welch and others take him to be.

In an interview conducted in 1977, for instance, Foucault reflects on the challenges the discovery of the Russian gulags posed for all socialist thought.[29] He declared that

> we must open our eyes...to what enables people there, on the spot, to resist the Gulag....We should listen to these people....What is it that sustains them, what gives them their energy, what is the force at work in their resistance, what makes them stand and fight?...The leverage against the Gulag is not in our heads, but in their bodies, their energy, what they say, think and do...there is indeed always something in the social body, in classes, groups, and individuals themselves which in some sense escapes relations of power....This measure...is not so much what stands outside relations of power as their limit, their underside, their counter-stroke, that which responds to every advance of power by a movement of disengagement. (136, 138)

Even though in the same breath Foucault adds that he opposes essentializing the people or invoking some doctrine of universal human rights, I find several features of this quotation counternihilistic. First, I detect an invariable commitment to basic principles that emerge again and again in Foucault's texts and that seem at least compatible with an ethic of reverence for lives. He repeatedly protests the subjugation, imprisonment, discipline, dissection, and further violation and abuse of human bodies. In his trenchant *Discipline and Punishment*, for instance, he turns Plato on his head by depicting how "the soul is the prison of the body."[30] And toward the end of his life he offered an interpretation of the Enlightenment that viewed it as upholding his own search for human freedom.[31] He speaks of the spirit of the *Aufklärung* as the promotion of a *"limit-attitude"* that leads to transgressions of the established orders on the part of those who possess "impatience for liberty" (45, 50, emphasis original).

If Foucault defies categorization as an ethical relativist, then, labeling him as the possessor of a sophistic view of reality may be rather exaggerated also. For his comments about the gulag display a perception of an anthropological constant, namely, something about the bodies and energies of members of the human species that always enables them to offer "counter-strokes" to and "disengagement" from dominant relations of power. Foucault's view of reality, then, in spite of its radical affirmation of historical contingency, seemingly maintains that no epistemes or disciplinary technologies can ever hold absolute sway. This theoretical construct appears to take the form, however reluctantly, of a quasi-universal claim about the nature of human history.[32]

By the same token I find a note of restrained optimism in Foucault's work. If in his view even Russian totalitarianism could not crush all resistance,[33] curiously enough the thinker who has done the most to uncover the pervasive presence of power in every dimension of human reality also provides warrants for refusing to despair about the genuine possibility of the success of movements for liberation. In her second book Welch's pessimism has been tempered by her refusal of "the evasion of the resiliency of our work for justice" (106). Yet she can still state that Habermas "claims, in contrast to Michel Foucault, that there is the possibility of significant social transformation and emancipation" (129). I would argue that on the sole basis of Foucault's perception of radical discontinuity in human history Welch's construction can be strenuously debated.[34]

There is another quotation from Foucault that raises questions about Welch's decision to base a theory of communicative incommensurability on an interpretation of his texts:

> There are times in life when the question of knowing if one
> can think differently than one thinks, and perceive differ-
> ently than one sees, is absolutely necessary if one is to go

on looking and reflecting at all...what is philosophy today — philosophical activity, I mean — if it is not the critical
work that thought brings to bear on itself? In what does it
consist, if not in the endeavor to know how and to what
extent it might be possible to think differently, instead of
legitimating what is already known?...[Philosophy] is entitled to explore what might be changed, in its own thought,
through the practice of a language [Fr. *Savoir*] that is foreign
to it....The studies that follow, like the others I have done
previously...[were] a philosophical exercise. The object was
to learn to what extent the effort to think one's own history
can free thought from what it silently thinks, and so enable
it to think differently.[35]

This statement possesses particular significance as a retrospec-
tive glance at his own work appearing in a book published the
year of Foucault's death (1984). And I find it difficult to rec-
oncile this thematization of his intellectual quest with Welch's
contention that the partiality of our logic and ethics can become
evident "only when that system is no longer our own." Foucault
here calls for a type of intellectual praxis whose rigorous demands
he has himself striven to satisfy, a "critical work thought brings
to bear on itself." The power of preconceived notions (what one
"silently thinks") is recognized, but at the same time I detect a refusal to accept these bonds in Foucault's references to strenuous
attempts to break through to that which is different. The objects
of this questioning gaze are not mental constructs already left be-
hind but one's "own thought" and one's "own history." Therein
resides the possibility of change, intimately related to our ability
to consider knowledge foreign to our own conceptualities.

Foucault's last work gives us a more specific indication of the
nature of this inquiring method that brings him rather close to
the orbit of rhetorical hermeneutics.[36] He says that though his
investigations "are not the work of a 'historian,'" they "are studies of 'history' by reason of the domain they deal with and the
references they appeal to" (9). His belief that some knowledge of
past systems of thought remains attainable distances his constructs
even further from the affirmation of absolute incommensurabil-

ity. For we must "examine both the difference that keeps us at
a remove from a way of thinking in which we recognize the
origins of our own, and the proximity that remains in spite of
that difference which we never cease to explore" (7). In regard
to knowledge of the past, then, Foucault hardly sounds like an
absolute skeptic.

I find his constant recourse to the record of the past in order to
unsettle established notions the most characteristic feature of Foucault's work as a whole. In the final phase of his scholarship[37] he
reconsidered the ethical legacy of Greek, Roman, and early Christian writers in order to show both how the Western construction
of ethical subjectivity emerged and how other paths could have
been taken. His knack for approaching the past in order to write
"the history of the present"[38] remains instructive for a study like
this one, which looks to textual artifacts in order to rhetorically
invent arguments useful for contemporary persuasive purposes.

And here the final contrast between Welch's work and my own
emerges. She refuses any attempt to ground her contentions on an
interpretation of Scripture or traditions.[39] The rationale for this
rejection of the religious past in toto is her belief that Christian
worldviews are radically flawed and directly responsible for modes
of thought that led to the death of millions of witches, Jews, and
other victims. Her historical judgments are often sweeping and
highly debatable,[40] but in any event she passes on the most fruitful
source of Foucault's argumentative instruments: the archive. Even
at his most radical Foucault accepted Western history as his own
and waged his battles from within, acknowledging his inescapable
location in that stream. Welch acknowledges the importance of
such realism about one's inevitable complicity,[41] and yet I do not
know which tradition she claims as her position in ongoing struggles. She rightly insists that Christian texts provide no infallible
foundation, but that is precisely the point: we must enter into the
ongoing fray of interpretation and argue for readings that fund
action in the defense of lives.[42]

I hope that I have by now established a case for believing that
rhetorical method distances itself from both epistemological and
moral relativism. Now I turn to the other pole and argue that
rhetoric must reject objectivism as well.

The Case Against Analytic Method

Boff defines analytical method as that which "produces demonstrative, or 'scientific,' lines of reasoning — not from general premises, but from first or basic principles, expressly defined."[43] Elsewhere in his book, particularly in the sections in which he retrieves the theology of Thomas Aquinas (70–78, for instance), Boff tells us from whence "first or basic principles" are derived: from an objective reality, which we perceive either through the data of our senses, through mental intuition, or via both working in concord.[44] This epistemological position is known under various names: *objectivism*, because truth has a status independent from individual knowers; *foundationalism*, because the central axioms form a reliable basis for all human knowing; *analytic*, because once the general principles are identified virtually all true knowledge can be deduced from them;[45] and *universalism*, because presumably anyone with sound mental and sensual faculties enjoys certain access to reality.

If unquestionable data were available to all hearers, what rhetorician would be so foolish as to fail to appeal to this most reliable of all persuasive resources? Our work would be made much less onerous, since we could dispense with all arguments based on character and emotion (except perhaps to clear away these obstructions blocking the view of truth)[46] and proceed directly to rational proofs graspable by the intelligent elite if not by the masses generally. But unfortunately Ciceronian rhetoric cannot subscribe to this worldview. This refusal does not base itself on the doubts about the existence of objective realities characteristic of sophistry, skepticism, and nihilism but only upon an awareness of human cognitive limits that prevent us from laying unmistakable hold upon the truth itself. In this section I wish to present the reasons rhetoricians and their allies have had for coming to this epistemological conclusion.

But first I must ask: does Boff himself subscribe to foundationalism? I find *Theology and Praxis* to render anything but an unambiguous verdict on this point. If the section entitled "The Process of Theoretical Praxis" (70–73) be taken as a hermeneutical key to the whole, I would construe his epistemology as follows:

there are "first generalities," objective raw data upon which concepts ("second generalities") then go to work in order to produce
(not discover) theories ("third generalities"). But the "first generalities" are described as "general, abstract, and ideological notions
that [one] encounters in a given culture" (71). In a way reminiscent
of the principle of decorum, then, Boff appears to point to social
and historical realities as his first principles. But I doubt whether
this is what Aristotle means by analytical method. Boff's concluding comments in this section seem to distance him decisively from
objectivist theories:

> At all events, it is absolutely imperative that we be rid of the
> "mirror myth of knowledge as the vision of a given object or
> the reading of an established text, neither of which is trans-
> parency itself."[47] Theoretical production must be understood
> for what it is: a practice of the production of cognition.
> (72–73)

Why then does he continue to insist on a rigid demarcation *between "analytical methodology"* and "heuristic practice...capable
of providing only a technology for rhetorical discourse" (77, emphasis original)? He appears to be looking for some way in which
liberationist claims can be accepted as something more than bare
assertions. His strategy involves the identification of various levels
of religious discourse. What he calls "spontaneous" and "undis-
ciplined" speech of faith (68) passes muster as effective popular
rhetoric, but it stands in need of the more rigorous grounding
characteristic of theology proper as defined by Boff. From the
perspective of the ethic of reverence for lives I find the following
quote particularly revealing:

> "The poor" do not go about with the words of revelation
> written all over their faces.... Accordingly, we must say that,
> taken in the immediacy of its formulation, the imperative
> that renders "life," and so forth, the *locus theologicus* par
> excellence is a failure as a guiding principle for the organiza-
> tion of theological discourse. At the same time, however, it
> must be acknowledged that such an imperative is not bereft
> of all "truth," even with respect to the theory of theology.

> The "truth" it holds must be carefully discerned, in order
> to be recognized — that is, that "an account be given" of
> this truth, that it be "rationalized," in terms of the *ratio*,
> the reason of which it is the "symptom," in all its empiricist
> wrappings. (176)

Boff may be arguing for communicative commensurability
here, and if so I have already stated my reasons for concurring
with him. But what strikes me as a non sequitur is his attendant
critique of rhetoric, which I must conclude can make sense only
on the basis of his two-level discourse theory. Yet he also shows
awareness of the analysis of language games pioneered by Ludwig
Wittgenstein (124–31). Since Wittgenstein believed that analytical
method represented a language game also, distinguished only by
its particular rules or "grammar," I am not surprised that Boff has
found it difficult to maintain his boundaries between "popular"
and "scientific" speech.[48] In more recent works he brings theology (no longer so narrowly defined) and religious life much closer
together.[49]

Boff himself, then, gives us good arguments for rejecting objectivism. I would posit the following additional reasons for
decisively rejecting this approach to epistemology.

1. Objectivism bases itself upon assertions, metaphors, and rhetorical warrants that defy the very rules of analytical deduction
that this philosophy of knowledge upholds. In the mid-nineteenth
century Søren Kierkegaard suggested that the entire edifice of
G. W. F. Hegel's massive philosophical system rested upon an un-
critical acceptance of its own notions of Actuality and Essence,
therefore falling into circular reasoning.[50] This attack on the pre-
tensions of objectivist theories was fiercely escalated by Friedrich
Nietzsche. His early linguistic reflections led him to the following
conclusion:

> But, it is not difficult to prove that what is called "rhe-
> torical," as a means of conscious art, had been active as a
> means of unconscious art in language and its development,
> indeed, that the *rhetorical is a further development*, guided
> by the clear light of the understanding, of *the artistic means
> which are already found in language*. There is obviously no

> unrhetorical "naturalness" of language to which one could
> appeal; language itself is the result of purely rhetorical arts
> ...*language is rhetoric*, because it desires to convey only a
> *doxa* [opinion], not an *episteme* [knowledge].[51]

Nietzsche based this conclusion on etymological considerations[52] that suggested the fact that a metaphor (and language is never "more" than metaphors in his view) arises in a particular situation but then is applied to other circumstances which cannot be equal. Meaning, or truth, is therefore simply convention, that which the users of words agree upon, persuaded by the rhetorical embellishments of language: "to be truthful means using the customary metaphors." But traditions change, so that Nietzsche speaks of a "mobile army of metaphors, metonyms, and anthropomorphisms."[53]

In later works Nietzsche argues that these clues sedimented in our philosophical discourse would expose the unscientific origin of our epistemological constructs if only we would perform rigorous linguistic and self-critique. But generally we, asleep in the forgetfulness of sloth or fear, take these very historical entities for granted as representations of objective realities. As a result every grand intellectual system has feet of clay, resting on assumptions that are nothing more than bare assertions.[54]

In order to adjudicate the justice of Nietzsche's anti-objectivist polemic, one can compare the previous paragraph with the summary of Aristotelian epistemology at the commencement of this section. Aristotle freely concedes that the first principles are not subject to rational or empirical demonstration but do not need to be, since reality offers them to us via our senses and our mental intuition. Nietzsche's challenge consists in this question: How can one be sure that axioms are not the legacy of human history, social convention, and the nature of "human, all too human" language instead?[55] Recent deconstructive operation upon the canonical texts of Western philosophy seems to have shifted the burden of proof back upon the foundationalists.[56] As noted previously, even the secure bastion of physical science has been shaken from within by practitioners who depict the operation of investigation as guided by overarching paradigms that gain assent

more through persuasion than strict demonstration. Obviously
one can claim that the anti-objectivists do not present an airtight
case either, but that is the point: every human quest for knowledge must begin with a "leap of faith" (Kierkegaard) and then give
the best warrants possible for that choice.

From this perspective one may begin to glimpse that universalist epistemology, which touted itself as a rejection of the vagaries
of rhetoric, has functioned as a powerful persuasive discourse in
the West. By convincing audiences that its method permitted certain access to truth, it gained a legitimacy that granted scientists of
all types enormous social prestige.[57] But how did the objectivists
wield their power?

2. Foundationalism enshrines particular interests and perspectives as universal truths. With the benefit of hindsight it has
become painfully apparent that the discoveries of the practitioners
of analytical methods in fields ranging from theology to biol-
ogy were often sophisticated expressions of the prejudices of their
epochs. By donning the mantle of objective truth the rhetoric of
antirhetorical epistemology thus had powerful ideological effects,
providing socially efficacious scientific legitimation to the ongoing
subjugation and exploitation of women, people of color, Jews, and
colonial populations.[58]

Historically contingent cultural presuppositions with lethal
consequences have thus accompanied claims of certain knowledge
at every step along the march of modernity. But does foundationalist epistemology inherently enable oppressive ideological praxis?
Haven't some proponents of feminism and civil rights employed
the very universalist discourse of the Enlightenment as leverage
against the perpetuation of a sexist and racist society?[59]

Foucault's analysis of human power would lead us to suspect
that every discourse generates resistances, but this fact should not
lead one to overlook the way in which foundationalism by definition involves what Theodor Adorno called a "logic of identity."[60]
Objectivism seeks after a limited set of unquestionable first principles from which all the rest of the edifice of knowledge can be
built by deduction, which is simultaneously reduction. Its quest
for essence, for a unitary conception of reality expressed in a to-
talizing epistemological system, cannot help but be uncomfortable

with a multitude of varying phenomena. Doctrines of knowledge therefore become techniques of mastery by which differences are repressed. Curiously, the affirmation of oneness thus always opens itself to the generation of dichotomies, for the universe can now be divided into two poles, that true to the essence of things and that which diverges from its norms.[61]

The speculations of that supposedly impractical pure discipline of philosophy, then, set the stage for the devaluation and control of social others. Here the rejection of the holistic anthropology of classical oratory also had fateful consequences. By taking the Platonic and Aristotelian distrust of the distorting effects of emotion and particular interests to extremes, Western thought construed subjectivity in exclusively intellectual terms, creating the ideal of the transcendental observer with a detached, impartial gaze. Persons who in actuality or in white male fantasies declined to share this version of fulfilled human existence were automatically relegated to inferior status. The "emotionalism" of women, the "inferior intelligence" of persons of African and Jewish descent, and the "fanaticism" of "Orientals" doomed them to perpetual minority under the tutelage of their Western fathers.

To put it mildly, then, analytical discourse has failed to live up to its promise. As Nietzsche predicted, the crumbling of modernist guarantees has led to widespread incredulity about all "metanarratives" (Lyotard), clearing a path for nihilism with concomitant political gridlock and social despair.[62] The history of modernism might well be summarized as the symbiosis of human knowing and human sinfulness.

The Epistemological Effects of Sin

The final comments of the previous section should offer a clue to a theological critique of antirhetorical epistemologies. Thus far in this chapter I have employed mostly extratheological lines of argument. Some critics might object that while I have made a case for a particular mode of secular reason, I have not established why rhetoric should so decisively shape the particular mode of rationality peculiar to systematic doctrinal reflection. Moreover, can't theology look to a special source of knowledge, namely, revelation? Doesn't God's gracious disclosure provide a much more certain foundation than the vagaries of persuasion?

It is no accident that the Augustinian tradition of rhetorical theology has also consistently taken human sinfulness seriously. In the next chapter I will attempt to correct the stereotypical estimation of this perspective as a bleak view of the human condition. I read this stream, running from Augustine through Luther and Calvin to Reinhold Niebuhr and beyond, as realistic, not pessimistic.[63] As Merold Westphal has suggested, this heritage of interpretation seeks to "take Paul seriously" — or perhaps more accurately, certain passages, such as Romans 7, understood in a particular fashion.[64]

But here too Christian theologians have followed Cicero's precedent. The orator wrote that we acquire "bad habits" almost from birth, and so "at once find ourselves in a world of iniquity amid a medley of wrong beliefs." As we mature we become progressively "infected with deceptions" until "truth gives place to unreality and the voice of nature to fixed prepossessions."[65] Both the pagan forebears and their Christian heirs, then, assumed that essential human nature should have permitted unsullied access to truth, but our historical reality always departs markedly from this ideal. We cannot transcend the fact of our corruption, blinded as we are by pride and selfishness. Calvin declared that it "is therefore in vain that so many burning lamps shine for us in the workmanship of the universe to show forth the glory of its Author." He chided the philosophers for "seeking in a ruin [i.e., fallen human nature] for a building and in scattered fragments for a well-knit structure."[66] Moreover, as I have already indicated, the practicality of the rhetorical ethos leads to a view of knowledge as that which enables action. And like Paul, the members of the Augustinian school have consistently insisted that even if we could see the truth clearly, vitiated by sin we are unable to act according to its dictates.

Many Christians seem to agree with this depiction of humans in their natural, pregrace state (cf. Romans 1–3). But once we have received God's revelation and been justified, don't we possess certain knowledge? The Augustinian school has insisted that "we walk by faith and not sight" (Hebrews 11) and that the Christian life is characterized by "fear and trembling" (Philippians 2:12). God's unfathomable mystery remains and is perhaps even deepened by our revelatory encounters with the divine "presence."[67] I have already noted that Calvin, for instance, conceived of the divine disclosure as a supreme act of persuasion. Correspondingly, faith is not the same as scientific or rational cognition. Calvin declared that "the knowledge of faith consists in assurance rather than in comprehension." He defined faith's epistemological status through the use of a key rhetorical term, as "solid constancy of persuasion," resulting in an attitude of "confidence" or loyalty (Latin *fiducia;* 3.2.14–15, pp. 560–61). As every rhetor knows, these are traits more characteristic of volition than of intellect. Calvin explicitly states that faith is "assent," which "is more of the heart than of the brain" (3.2.8, p. 552).[68]

Finally, as most people know, the Augustinian tradition insists that sin continues to afflict Christians as long as we live. With typical rhetorical flourish Calvin spoke of the ever-present and "continuing occasion for struggle" against that remaining "smoldering cinder of evil" (3.3.10, p. 602). As Westphal has demonstrated (p. 213), this insistence on "total depravity" refers to extension, not degree. I would suggest that in human life, including its Christian variety, there are no safe bases where sin cannot tag us. Epistemology therefore cannot constitute a sin-free haven either. We are indeed, as the Heideggerian motto proclaims, confined to the "prison house of language" where we may be persuaded but never absolutely sure of the truth.

But there is much we can do to make our dwelling a better place for human flourishing. If rhetoric is all we have, it represents a useful tool for our betterment. In the next chapter I seek to conclude my case for theology as rhetorical hermeneutics by offering an illustration of that prospect.

CHAPTER FOUR

Rhetorical Hermeneutics and the Christian Doctrine of Sin Today

To conclude my case for rhetorical theological method, I will attempt to illustrate how this approach to hermeneutics would shape the formulation of a particular traditional locus for theological reflection. Since in the last chapter I suggested that the Christian doctrine of human sinfulness supports the limited epistemological claims of persuasive discourses, in this final chapter I will further develop a rhetorical construction of a contemporary theology of sin.

The State of Contemporary Theological Reflection on Sin

Recall that the first step of Steven Mailloux's method involves the need to distinguish one's own interpretation from that others have given of the same subject. I begin, then, with a brief survey of recent contributions to the Christian doctrine of sin.

I have been surprised to note that on the North Atlantic intellectual scene the doctrine of sin, technically known as hamartiology, has become the least popular subject of dogmatic monographs. Indeed, any interested student could easily become familiar with the handful of recent scholarly works by Protestant authors.[1] In spite of the multiplicity of manifestations of human evil in the twentieth century, virtually all of these works devote themselves to tracing broad anthropological constants.[2] Rather than devoting themselves to an analysis vitally linked to our contemporary problems, systematicians pursue something akin to what Edward Farley terms "reflexive ontology." Merold Westphal typifies their mutual approach when he states that he hopes to achieve "the art of understanding" the essence of our human condition. Thus even Roger Haight, one of the dogmaticians addressing social sin, presents "an analytical, descriptive account of the meaning of these doctrines" and insists that the social variety, too is "not personal or actual sinning but an existential propensity toward it."[3] In light of those texts comprising the resources of Scripture and Christian traditions, I find this consistent narrowing of the subject in recent scholarship odd. I will argue for the prevalence of the theme of actual sins in canonical sources, and given that legacy the virtually exclusive focus on original sin in contemporary theology — when the topic of human evil is considered at all — requires some explanation.

For this delimitation of hamartiology does not characterize the worldwide theological scene. At least since the Second Latin American Episcopal Conference, meeting in Medellín, Colombia, in 1968, denounced the specific sins of economic dependency and institutionalized violence, liberation theologians in the Americas, including practitioners of black and feminist theologies, have employed the social sciences and philosophy to focus on the actual effects of human evil in their contexts.[4] Their work has had considerable impact on the direction of North Atlantic "malestream" theology[5] and has decisively influenced the present study. Why then have we not seen a corresponding change in the bearing of hamartiology?[6] To answer this question I will pursue the second step of Mailloux's method, namely, that of situating the particular acts of interpretation within relevant institutional discourses.

The Institutional Context of Theology in North America

Attention to the academic setting of theology in the United States may provide clues useful to the positing of hypotheses accounting for the present state of the hamartiological question here. In his insightful work, appropriately entitled *Whatever Became of Sin?*,[7] the psychiatrist Karl Menninger pointed to diverse evidence demonstrating the almost complete disappearance from our cultural scene of the word and the concepts it signified. Menninger explained this shift with reference to the inroads of secularization: the courts redefine wrong acts as crimes, while psychologists and sociologists submit symptoms to a causal analysis that renders the assignment of guilt obsolete. But Menninger also chides religious leaders for surrendering their still-considerable ethical authority by meekly accepting their relegation to the margins of modern society, failing to use the pulpit to indict wrongdoing or issue calls for repentance. From my perspective as a participant in theological education this latter reality requires an explanation going beyond Menninger's appeal to the effects of secularization on clerical mentality. Put differently, the critical question seems to be: Why were religious leaders persuaded by arguments advocating turning the management of sin over to other social agents?

The fateful decision to follow the standards of professionalization in theological education undoubtedly played a key role. For the dominant standards of the helping professions would undergird precisely the clinicalization of sin described by Menninger. Moreover, the pursuit of narrow disciplinary specialization has worked to distance both theologians and the clergy they train from the public arena where issues like inner-city violence and global warming are at the center of the discussion.[8]

But there's more to the story. In fact, we may be witnessing an apt illustration of one of the leading motifs of classical Christian reflection on human sinfulness: good intentions gone wrong. My rather unscientific survey based on data from my own experience and that of colleagues would suggest that conscientious pastoral workers lamented the tremendous abuses that resulted from prevalent articulations of the doctrine of sin. Encounters with battered women, for instance, revealed how traditional affirmations could encourage psychic destructiveness and the continuation of oppression.[9] A contemporary rhetorical approach to the theology of sin, then, must pay serious attention to the critiques of hamartiology. In doing so I begin to address Mailloux's third concern, namely, the importance of embedding acts of interpretation within prevailing cultural practices and social and material circumstances.

The Virtuosi of Suspicion and Their Critique of Christian Hamartiology

Training in the humanities exposed many Christian readers to the withering attacks of writers Paul Ricoeur has called the "masters of suspicion:" Karl Marx, Friedrich Nietzsche, and Sigmund

Freud.[10] In recent years the feminist Mary Daly has made a similar impact, so that I would propose the more inclusive term "virtuosi of suspicion." Each of these influential thinkers explicitly or implicitly rejected the Christian conception of sin. A brief reflection on a scathing passage from Marx's *The Holy Family*[11] may indicate the tenor of this type of denunciation.

Marx performs his brand of rhetorical literary criticism on a French novel by Eugene Sue entitled *Fleur de Marie*. Marie is a poor matchgirl who against her will is sold into the bondage of prostitution at a criminal's brothel. In spite of her horrible victimization she retains her childlike innocence and "can...put up a fight" (168). Moreover,

> contrary to Christian *repentance*... *Good* and *evil*, as Marie conceives them, are not the *moral abstractions* of good and evil. She is *good* because she has never caused *suffering* to anyone, she has always been *human* towards her *inhuman* surroundings. She is *good* because the sun and the flowers reveal to her her own sunny and blossoming nature.... Her situation is *not good*, because it puts an unnatural constraint on her, because it is not the expression of her human impulses,... because it is full of torment and without joy. (169–70)

After this promising start Marx accuses Sue of opting to "atone for his temerity" by turning Marie over to the establishment in the form of its "current religion" (170). Though she loves God in her own way, the priest Laporte rapidly "bestows on her the *consciousness of her sins*." He "must soil her in her own eyes, he must trample underfoot her natural, spiritual resources" (171–72) in order to induce her to accept Christian baptism. Marie realizes now that she "had been more guilty than unfortunate." She even thanks God for "the Christian and hence unbearable consciousness of eternal damnation.... From this moment Marie is *enslaved by the consciousness of sin*... and continual hypochondriacal self-torture... becomes her duty" (173–74).

Burdened by this infinite debt, Marx reports, Marie becomes a nun, then a prioress, but "her Christian consolation is pre-

cisely annihilation of her real life and essence — her death."
And so she concludes her tragic metamorphosis from victim to
"repentant sinner" to "corpse" (175–76). Glimmerings of what
Nietzsche would later call the fatal "illness... of bad conscience,"[12]
what Freud diagnosed as the "death instinct,"[13] and what Daly
excoriates as the misogynist "necrophilia"[14] of patriarchal Christian faith are already visible in this artifact from Marx's early
career (1845).

Faced with such challenges, Christian theologians might respond in several ways. First, one may ignore the critiques as
misguided and inconsequential. But in my judgment the internal
dynamics of Christian faith invalidate such facile dismissal. As I
indicated previously, in our century Albert Schweitzer identified
the core of the gospel with what he called the "ethics of reverence for life." This led him to propose a definition of good and
evil quite similar to the one Marx approves at the beginning of
his reading of Sue's novel: "Good is: preserving and furthering
life; bad is: impeding and destroying life."[15] Any charge suggesting
that the doctrine of sin has collaborated with the forces of death
therefore deserves the serious attention of Christian theologians.

A second option would entail ceasing to speak of sin. Perhaps
this rationale might partially account for the studious neglect of
hamartiology by most North Atlantic theologians. But even if one
avoids the terminology of sin, the tragic manifestations of human
evil in this age will lead to the emergence of the same subject in
different guises. As Jean Delumeau writes in the introduction to
his massive history of the Western guilt culture: "Our era con-
stantly speaks about liberating itself from guilt feelings without
noticing that, in the entire history of guilt, the accusation of
others has never been as strong as it is today."[16] In fact the power
of the discourses articulated by the virtuosi of suspicion lies in
their indictment of ecclesial beliefs and practices that have actively
contributed to the oppression of others: they consider hamartiology a sin. The fact that the doctrine of sin has been distorted,
then, argues in favor of its reformulation, not its abandonment.
Don't the very tenets of traditional hamartiology lead one to expect that such abuses can always occur? And by the same token,
what guarantees exist to assure that the new secular experts on

human evil will steadily succeed in avoiding the malevolence of the will to power?

Proponents of a third alternative, then, attempt to arrive at a new understanding of hamartiology more consonant with modern sensibilities. Their proposals must first describe the errors of the traditional formulations and then propose a solution appropriate to their diagnosis. The limited number of recent North Atlantic contributions to the doctrine of sin all belong to this category. The manner in which these theologians have performed this task, however, further demonstrates the constraints imposed by their institutional and social locations.

A Critique of Standard Accounts of Christian Hamartiology

Robert Williams's essay on sin and evil in a popular text edited by Peter Hodgson and Robert King may be considered as a typical illustration of the now standard theological approach to human sinfulness.[17] Williams begins by examining what he refers to as "*the* scriptural legacy" concerning sin, namely, Genesis 2–3 and Paul's reformulation of this tradition in Romans 5:12–21. As he sees it these sources illumine "the anthropological origin of evil" (196–98, emphasis added). Then he devotes considerable space to St. Augustine's teaching, which he considers the epitome of the "classical formulation" (196). Whereas many followers of the school Williams represents focus only on Augustine's so-called final position,[18] at least Williams acknowledges temporal stages in the development of the saint's views. First he discusses Augustine's anti-Manichaean phase, when he defended the goodness of creation by speaking of sin as a contingent reality introduced by human freedom but without ontological status. And then he describes the anti-Pelagian writings, when Augustine stressed the character of sin as a profound corruption of human nature affecting all members of our species. Harmonizing these two motifs into a complex unitary structure of thought, Williams sees the later contributions of Thomas Aquinas and the Reformers as mere elaborations on this foundation.

Having opted to view the Augustinian position (=the doc-

trine of original sin) in a systematic light, in Williams's eyes it must appear unavoidably contradictory. One critical issue concerns human accountability: As Hendrikus Berkhof expresses the paradox, is sin fate or guilt? Another perceived incongruity involves human procreation within a good creation: if original sin is somehow passed on from generation to generation, isn't bodily desire unavoidably evil? As some feminists argue, don't women then become inherently suspect, since they play the preponderant role in the process of birth?[19]

Williams suggests that to overcome these drawbacks the Augustinian position must either be restated or abandoned. He describes several attempts to do that. One might relocate the inheritance of sin either in an anthropological depth structure or in the social realm. Thus Reinhold Niebuhr depicts the state of anxiety facing all human beings and the potential for sin residing in inappropriate responses to our finitude.[20] Piet Schoonenberg, however, retrieves the biblical concept of the "sin of the world" to point to the disorders of the sociocultural realm that precede the choices made by any particular individual.[21] The contributions of John Hick and Paul Ricoeur claim to offer alternatives to the dominant Western framework. Hick's so-called Irenaean paradigm eschews the idea of a fall, preferring to portray human beings as weak and immature creatures who must grow into the stature of Christ through their encounters with evil.[22] Ricoeur laments Augustine's attempt to turn evocative myths into logically consistent theological concepts, and practices a phenomenology of the diverse core symbols emerging from penitential reflection on the human experience of evil as defilement, sin, and guilt.[23]

This third response to the challenge of the virtuosi presupposes a fundamental methodological commitment shared by virtually all contemporary theologians: our doctrinal formulations must be appropriate to our context and an adequate interpretation of the texts of the Christian past. In other words, as I insisted at the outset, good theology must be measured by the criteria of relevance and identity. But I contend that this particular construal of relevance has led to a series of distorted images of classical doctrines of sin (to suggest that any one paradigm, such as Augustinianism, became dominant is itself a distortion). In my judgment the use of sources typified by Williams excludes both alternative interpretations of the material included and numerous other relevant texts. I therefore offer an alternative interpretation below.

I do not wish to suggest that Williams and his colleagues have engaged in deliberate acts of caricature. It seems far more probable that their textual interpretation results from their adherence to a particular theoretical grid, a way of seeing profoundly influenced by adherence to a dominant scholarly paradigm. For like most theologians in the modern era, Williams works in a university setting. In the wake of the Enlightenment critiques of religion, this discipline has been required to struggle in order to maintain its academic location and credibility alongside other sciences. As David Klemm contends, the "primary audience of theology is the university community, and it is primarily answerable to the standards of that community."[24]

Debate is currently raging about exactly what those standards should be, and this breakdown of methodological consensus undermines the confidence scholars need to engage in public debates.[25] Until a new consensus emerges, academics will tend, albeit unconsciously, to fall back into the old ways. And before the onset of postmodernism the canons of what the Frankfurt School termed "positive science" dominated.[26] In brief, the aim of academics was therefore the production of knowledge as an end in itself. To attain the stature of scientific knowledge, a theory had to be capable of generalizability, that is, it must show how a variety of data could be accounted for through a single conceptual principle. Second, according to the principle of causality, a theory was required to explain how the current configuration of sense data came to acquire its present shape.

In light of such principles the preoccupation of modern hamartiology with the question of original sin seems less mysterious. Naturally this abstract, universal description of a static human state offered theoretical coherence that concentration on actual faults might impede.[27] By the same token it is no wonder that, as Menninger perceived, sin becomes increasingly identified with fate, not personal responsibility. Above all, however, one may appreciate why sin represents not a moral but an intellectual problem, a question not of actions but of meaning.[28] The fate of hamartiology today, then, mirrors the state of systematic theology as a whole — itself a reflection of wider academic trends.

Toward Hamartiology as Critical Theory

As I begin to offer my alternative, I must first retrace Mailloux's second and third steps in order to provide the context for my own act of interpretation.

The discipline of theology that I also represent owes a debt of gratitude to scientific theology, for its adaptation to the requirements of the modern academy accomplished its goal of preserving a voice in the university for our discipline. But I align myself with those who believe that today theologians increasingly face different demands both internal and external to the academy. Relevance can no longer be defined primarily in terms of apologetics aimed at the practitioners of a certain brand of higher education. I am particularly concerned about the cogency of theology as the pursuit of understanding in the light of the massive suffering of our age and the resulting voices of protest so ably articulated by the virtuosi of suspicion.

Human history has known many atrocities, but few would rival the bloody horrors of our age. All told, in "excess of 100,000,000 have been killed by human violence in the wars and revolutions of the twentieth century."[29] But regrettably, state-sponsored lethal force narrates only a small portion of the tale of our times. About 40,000 young children, congregated primarily in the so-called Third World, die preventable deaths every day "as a result of severe nutritional stress and infectious diseases."[30] Moreover, in the final decade of the twentieth century it becomes ever harder to deny that human productive and reproductive performance poses a growing threat to our ecosystem's continued ability to sustain future human generations.[31] Ecological devastation already accounts for a shocking annual death toll. Some believe that as many as 100,000 children succumb to pollution in Mexico City every year,[32] and "ozone depletion is expected to cause 3 million to 15 million new cases [of skin cancer] in Americans born before 2075; some 52,000 to 252,000 of those patients are likely to die from the disease."[33] Just at the moment when the Cold War should lift the anxiety occasioned by the threat of thermonuclear annihilation, the human race faces yet another prospect for extinction due to global warming while the heralds of the new world order refuse to exert leadership.[34]

For many citizens of the United States, however, it is difficult to focus on the global crisis when the impairment, if not extinction, of life hits so many of them perilously close to or in their home. Alarmingly, at present in the United States almost "one out of every two women will become a victim of completed or attempted rape in her lifetime." The statistics on the violent abuse of children are equally horrifying.[35] Scores of individuals — mostly young, poor, from our inner cities, and representing an ethnic minority — are killed every year by handguns whose possession would be denied to them in most civilized countries.[36]

How should contemporary Christian theologians respond to these terrors and many others one might have mentioned? Like so many of my theological contemporaries, I began by raising questions about God through the pursuit of "the problem of evil."[37] Eventually, however, I found this line of inquiry to be a dead end. As Immanuel Kant cogently argued long ago, the mystery of evil will not yield to an intellectual solution but only to a moral response.[38] Consequently too much speculation about divinity or the order of things can become an excuse by which humans overlook the fact that we are the agents responsible for creating and maintaining all of the problems to which I have alluded.[39]

If anthropodicy must therefore replace theodicy, the phenomena of human-caused suffering seem to require not general notions about God, humans, or the anthropological basis of sinfulness but a type of hamartiology that can analyze and denounce the specific evils we face. I therefore concur with those who believe that maintaining relevance requires a shift of paradigms. To engage in prophetic hamartiology today, then, one must propose different approaches to theological method.

Consider, for instance, Marx's famous thesis on Feuerbach: "The philosophers have only *interpreted* the world, in various ways; the point is to *change* it."[40] If practitioners of hamartiology wish to respond to his critique, then, they must consider ways in which the doctrine of sin and theology as a whole might function as a critical theory of society. As Raymond Geuss summarizes this approach, such heuristic constructs seek to serve as "guides for human action" and "are aimed at producing enlightenment in the agents who hold them, i.e. at enabling those agents to determine what their true interests are." Consequently they are "inherently emancipatory" (1–2). In other words, critical theory does not pursue objective knowledge as such but offers a pragmatic diagnosis that aims to loosen the readers' allegiance to the oppressive status quo.

If this option is chosen the Christian doctrine of sin can operate not primarily to understand sin but rather to overcome the negative effects of concrete sins. As always, this will require attention to both identity and relevance. Following the common distinction in Latin American liberation theology between "hermeneutical mediation" and "socio-analytic mediation," I believe theologians need to articulate both critical theories of reading and critical theories of society.[41] In practice, however, the two tasks always overlap. For texts are always read from the perspective of a particular horizon, and one's perception of the current horizon is also shaped by formation in the particular narratives of a textual tradition.[42]

Nonetheless I approach hamartiology here beginning from the perspective of "hermeneutical mediation."[43] In the next section I suggest that Christianity has its own resources for critical hamartiology: the prophetic traditions. I wish to argue that the recovery of that strand offers prospects for the forging of alliances with those followers and traveling companions of the virtuosi struggling to effect social transformation in the hope of forestalling the perpetuation of mechanisms of mass death. I am concerned here with the question of how one can with integrity interpret the textual treatments of sin in the Christian past in such a way as to fund praxis on behalf of human flourishing. I would need a whole book to make that case fully, but I hope that the following reflections will at least point the way.

A Brief Reinterpretation of the Traditions of Christian Hamartiology

Beginning with the Bible, it is by no means certain that Genesis 2–3 and Romans 5 must be read as reflections on the origin of human evil. Williams himself points to Paul's overriding soteriological purpose, and Ricoeur, his mentor for the reinterpretation of the myth of Adam and Eve, has suggested that this story may reflect the experience of exile — a view consonant with the refusal of Jewish interpreters to find a basis there for the doctrine of original sin.[44] Since even Berkhof admits that there are no unmistakable references to the saga of Eden anywhere else in the Hebrew Scriptures (205), could it be that biblical writers weren't very interested in the question of sin's origin?

I contend that if one must speak of the biblical view of sin, the overwhelming preponderance of the material would point to the reconstruction of what I call the prophetic tradition, since its most sustained expression is found in the writings of the preexilic Judean prophets. Perusing the brief book of Amos of Tekoa gives one an adequate representation of the discourse of this school. Their doctrine of sin involves accusing society of specific behavioral violations of the covenant established by the gracious Yahweh, a constitution requiring respect for deity and just treatment of neighbors. In this schema transgression occurs in specific historical acts that aren't so much described as indicted. General questions of causality are secondary, provided they are of any interest.

Moreover, this prophetic strain survived in the New Testament. Luke in particular frequently portrays Jesus as a Hebrew prophet; see, for instance, his version of the Beatitudes that appends the "woes" (Luke 6:20–26). Moreover, writings such as 1 John, James, and Revelation (especially chapter 18) would appear indispensable to any rounded discussion of biblical hamartiology. Even in the Pastorals, which supposedly reflect the church's growing willingness to accommodate to the existing social order, one finds this concise definition: "the love of money is the root of all evils" (1 Timothy 6:10). Thomas Aquinas followed the patristic precedent by taking this statement with great seriousness.[45] Yet I have located not one single reference to it in recent North Atlantic treatments of human sinfulness.

Turning to postbiblical texts one finds the same pattern repeated. John Chrysostom's denunciation of the rich represents only one important source overlooked by Williams and others.[46]

But their interpretation of Augustine must also be contested. I consider it erroneous to suggest that the bishop of Hippo wished to propound anything like a modern systematic theology. All his writings were occasional, addressing themselves to current controversies. He tells us himself that before his conversion he was a professional teacher of rhetoric.[47] I have already discussed his great rhetorical textbook, *On Christian Doctrine*. Since rhetors, as we have seen, aim each treatise at specific and ever different audiences, contradictions between various texts are to be expected, and the so-called inconsistencies in Augustine's thought become less problematic.

But the standard accounts of the Augustinian position on human sinfulness also fail to tell the whole story. First, Augustine also represents the prophetic tradition. In the bulky *City of God* he displays all of imperial Rome's "glittering vices" in lurid detail.[48] Second, a careful rereading of the anti-Pelagian texts that Williams, Haight, and Berkhof believe to be the definitive statements of Augustine's mature position makes one wonder about their construal of his intent. Perusal of just a few statements in *On the Grace of Christ and Original Sin*[49] may suggest other interpretive possibilities.

Defending the necessity for grace-monism — Augustine's primary concern seems to be the implications Pelagian hamartiology would have on the doctrine of grace — the saint declares that "as strength is made perfect in weakness, whoever does not own himself to be weak, is not in the way to be perfected." And in what does perfection consist? "By such grace it is effected, not only that we discover what ought to be done, but also that we do what we have discovered" (1.13, p. 592) — a typical rhetorical concern. Seemingly what is at stake, then, is not so much true doctrinal comprehension but the possibility of sanctification. And a holy Christian life is characterized by the same kind of charity God revealed through unmerited prevenient grace. Augustine claims that "in order, indeed, that we might receive that love whereby we might love, we were loved while as yet we had no love in ourselves" (1.27, p. 602).

More is at stake here then correct perception of Augustine's meaning. Modern theology has generally accepted St. Anselm's

Augustinian definition of theology, "faith seeking understanding."[50] But if my reading in the preceding paragraph be accepted, can one maintain that Augustine considered understanding an end in itself? Or does another conclusion seem warranted, namely, that the purpose of right ideas (orthodoxy) is to enable right actions (orthopraxis)? I am convinced that, akin to many other Christian authors, Augustine utilized doctrine as an instrument in the rhetorical formation of Christian persons who practiced love. Such considerations suggest the need for a thorough reassessment of the Augustinian doctrine of original sin.

I don't possess the expertise in the study of late antiquity required for such reinterpretation, but I feel confident enough to offer a brief account of the hamartiology of one of Augustine's principal heirs, John Calvin. As Justo González points out, in the popular mind the Reformer is most often associated with two doctrines: predestination and a pessimistic view of the human condition.[51] Yet no one has devoted a thorough and comprehensive scholarly monograph to his views on human sinfulness.[52] Williams exemplifies a resulting tendency to conclude that Calvin's hamartiology follows the basic outline of the Augustinian model. Closer examination of the *Institutes*, however, reveals a rather different picture.

Handbooks usually point to the opening chapters of book 2 as Calvin's definitive statement on human sinfulness. If we took these brief and unremarkable statements to be an adequate summary of his hamartiology, we might safely conclude that he fits the Augustinian stereotype — though his lack of interest in the origin of sin might give pause. But Calvin has far more to say about human evil.

First the purpose of Calvin's major theological work should be understood. And as expected from the hand of a rhetorical writer, its goals do not coincide with those of modern scholarly theology. In his dedicatory preface to his *Commentary on the Psalms* (1557), Calvin recalls that while he was in exile at Basel,

> a great fire of hatred [for France] had been kindled in Germany by the exile of many godly men [sic] from France. To quench this fire, wicked and lying rumors were spread, cru-

elly calling the exiles Anabaptists and seditious men, men who threatened to upset, not only religion, but the whole political order with their perverse madness. I saw that this was a trick of those in [the French] court, not only to cover up with false slanders the shedding of innocent blood of holy martyrs, but also to enable the persecutors to continue with the pitiless slaughter. Therefore I felt that I must make a strong statement against such charges; for I could not be silent without treachery. This was why I published the Institutes — to defend against unjust slander my brothers [sic] whose death was precious in the Lord's sight. A second reason was my desire to rouse the sympathy and concern of people outside, since the same punishment threatened many other poor people.[53]

To defend his coreligionists Calvin followed a tripartite method of rhetorical hermeneutics. He offered an interpretation of human experience, of the traditions of the church, and especially of the Holy Scriptures. But the theological contestations are supplemented by explicit political polemics. These become especially numerous in book 4, perhaps the portion dogmaticians have appreciated the least. After outlining his plan for the fourth book Calvin states: "At the same time we are to call back godly readers from those corruptions by which Satan, in the papacy, has polluted everything God had appointed for our salvation" (4.1.1, p. 1012). Much as it may embarrass contemporary ecumenical sensibilities, Calvin's prophetic hamartiology represents an all-out assault on the papal regime, which he believed to lie at the root of the troubles of his age. Most of what he has to say about human sinfulness, then, assumes the form of specific indictments.

Calvin's concrete critiques of the late medieval papacy may be summarized in terms of three key themes: the violation of neighbors; tyranny as shored up by idolatry; and the abuse of confession and penitence.

1. Calvin's understanding of the content of the law follows the rule laid down by Jesus' famous summation: "we should love the Lord our God with all our heart, and with all our soul, and with all our powers" and "we should love our neighbor as ourselves"

(Luke 10:27; Matthew 22:37, 39 as cited in 2.8.11, p. 377). Eschewing an individualistic interpretation of the second half, Calvin claims that it dictates how "we ought to conduct ourselves in human society."

Why? Because every person "is both the image of God, and our flesh." Hence "we ought to hold our neighbor sacred," and "we ought to cherish his [sic] as our own flesh" (2.8.39–40, pp. 404–5).

Both the social cast of Calvin's thought and his defense of human lives by granting them a share of God's honor become more apparent as he considers the eighth commandment, "You shall not steal." He begins by establishing that "injustice is an abomination to God." He continues by suggesting that theft takes many forms, including "hard and inhuman laws with which the more powerful oppresses and crushes the weaker person" and the master who "savagely harasses his household." Due obedience to this command must therefore involve the refusal "to become wealthy through injustice" or to "heap up riches cruelly wrung from the blood of others." In Calvin's vision the various vocations in human society (magistracy, ministry, parenthood) exist "to protect and promote the well-being and interest of others," and failure to perform one's assigned duty constitutes robbery (2.8.45–46, pp. 408–11). Calvin consistently equates luxurious living, a violation of the stewardship entrusted to us by divine kindness, with the absence of charity. In his chapter on Christian freedom (3.19.9, pp. 840–42) he therefore warns that the liberty of the gospel does not give one license to lead an extravagant lifestyle.

Such a sampling of passages should show how consistently Calvin protests against the violation and abuse of human persons, and they point to the extraordinary boldness of the strategy employed to that end: equating sins against humans with sacrilege against the supreme ruler of heaven and earth. Calvin claims that in gazing upon mortal creatures God "sees in them the marks and features of his own countenance." Therefore, wherever God contemplates "his [sic] own face, he both rightly loves it and holds it in honor" (3.17.5, p. 807).

Having established this fundamental ethical principle, Calvin turns it into a slashing critique of then-current papal practice as he perceived it. He condemns papal government as "a robber's den in which thieves riot." Via simony sacred offices are up for sale, and everyone can buy shares in a lucrative but shady profit-taking scheme (4.5.13, p. 1096; cf. 4.5.4–10, pp. 1087–95). Not only does such behavior amount to "slitting the church's throat," but also from false deacons "the poor get nothing more of those alms than if they were cast into the sea" (4.5.15, p. 1098).

Far less than the quarter of church income designated in ancient ecclesial canons reaches paupers, and Calvin asserts that the portion assigned to them should be far larger, for the discretionary funds of the bishops as well as wealth assigned to buildings and furnishings "ought to be made available to the poor in time of need." In harmony with his treatment of the law Calvin can thus charge the Roman clergy with both theft and sacrilege (4.5.16, pp. 1098–99). For "so far are they from taking due care of living temples that they would rather let many thousands of the poor die of hunger than break the smallest cup or cruet to relieve their need." The excessive "adornment of churches" (4.5.18, p. 1100) fills Calvin with disgust. And he is outraged that "those whom God's eternal and inviolable decree forbids to be seekers of filthy lucre, and bids be content with simple fare" have deigned "not only to lay hands on villages and castles, but to carry off vast provinces, finally to seize whole kingdoms!" (4.5.19, p. 1101).

I find Calvin's metaphor of the image of God and the specific way that it surfaces in his campaign against ecclesial injustice most suggestive in today's context. It offers resources for articulating the dignity of all human persons for religious audiences, for in the fashion of the Hebrew prophets he depicts God's personal offense when the rights of neighbors are trampled under foot. And in book 4 he retrieves biblical and patristic themes to construct a case that in striking ways resembles the emphases on God's preferential option for the poor and the voluntary poverty of the church that have emerged from Latin American liberation theology. If one concurs in his judgment that the persistence of poverty represents theft and sacrilege, the structural deprivation of at least two-thirds of humanity in our time should lead to serious questioning and reform of the ongoing economic praxis of our churches and our society.

2. Calvin's harsh view of the late medieval papacy is also based

on his strong aversion to arbitrary power in human affairs. He seems to realize, for instance, that one hallmark of despotism is its tendency to globally apply an institution useful only for a particular locality. Calvin insists that "no one person is competent to rule" over "the whole earth" (4.6.8, p. 1109). The true church "has Christ as its sole head" (4.6.9, p. 1110), and true ecclesiastical unity is found not in human governance but "in God and in faith in Christ" (4.6.10, p. 1111).

Calvin's awareness of the ever-present possibility of human perversity influences his opposition to absolutism. He admires the way in which in the early church bishops of Rome both admonished and were rebuked by their episcopal colleagues (4.7.7, pp. 1125–26). But now the popes "leave no jurisdiction on earth to control or restrain their lust if they abuse such boundless power." Since they are accountable to no one, the pontiffs are free to "exercise tyranny over God's people" and to "turn the pastoral office into robbery" (4.7.19, pp. 138–39). Calvin concludes: "if we simply grant to men [sic] such power as they are disposed to take, it is plain to all how abrupt is the fall into tyranny, which ought to be far from Christ's church" (4.8.1, p. 1150).

But Calvin goes beyond denunciations of the abuse of power to offer an analysis of the ways in which its wielders legitimate their questionable authority. Many commentators have noted the key role that the trope of idolatry performs in Calvin's work of "unmasking."[54] But that this emphasis functions as a kind of critique of ideology has rarely been noted. True, God's honor is at stake, but so is human dignity. Thus Calvin begins his prosecution by mentioning the "foulest sacrilege" of the Mass, the perversion of worship by a "mass of superstitions," and the conversion of public assemblies into "schools of idolatry." But he also speaks of these deviations as "lies" that "snare us." In the same exordium, then, he also offers a preview of the arguments his opponents use to justify their "perverse government." One receives the impression that idolatry serves an instrumental purpose in the papal enterprise: "their one purpose is to defend their own cause in any way they can without regard for truth" (4.2.2, pp. 1042–43). Hence Calvin's rhetorical contestation of their textual practice and his denunciation of idolatry proceed along the same lines.

For the misdirected rites, too, operate persuasively, convincing the religious that their salvation depends upon that which only the Roman church can offer.

Addressing the misuse of church funds, then, Calvin alleges that the clerics "induce the people by superstition to apply what should have been distributed to the poor, to the constructing of churches, erecting statues, buying vessels, and providing sacred vestments. Thus are daily alms consumed in this abyss" (4.5.18, p. 1101). And to defend its tyranny the apostolic see usurps the place of God; its claims to infallibility "carry the force of oracles." Its theologians and canonists are ever ready to twist traditions or come up with forged evidence in order to "flatter their idol" (4.7.20, p. 1140). Instead of depositing sole trust in God's word, "they would have our faith stand and fall on their decision" (4.8.10, p. 1159).

Once more these old statements possess a certain contemporary resonance. For the experiences of Women-Church and the Latin American base communities indicate that authority must emerge "from below," going beyond mere consent to choices handed down "from above." But I find the link Calvin established between idolatry and domination and his recognition of the persuasive power of images and rites particularly suggestive in the late twentieth century. Guided by this precedent, today's rhetorical hamartiology might therefore wish to utilize the work of those who claim that our ecologically destructive and murderously inequitable "world economic order" perpetuates itself via the eloquence of quasi-religious "mystifications" (Burke). Doing the doctrine of sin involves daring rhetorical critique that discovers the unquestioned and questionable assumptions that permit a destructive system to continue.

3. The late medieval doctrine of sin that funded the sacrament of confession and absolution was particularly abhorrent to Calvin, and he devotes a considerable amount of space to a refutation of it in books 3 and 4. In these sections his talent for invective is on full display. For in his mind "the most serious matter of all is under discussion: namely forgiveness of sins." Unless we know how it may be obtained, "the conscience can have no rest at all, no peace with God, no assurance or security" (3.4.2, pp. 624–25). In fact the

true church may be characterized as that place where "sins have been and are daily pardoned" (4.1.21, p. 1035). The Roman hierarchy, then, is grievously at fault for not only failing to promote, but also obstructing this most salutary work.

Calvin lamented the way in which the priests laid emphasis upon the necessity of enumerating all of one's sins in the confessional. How could anyone be sure that they had satisfactorily fulfilled this requirement? Calvin's central theological move involves shifting one's gaze away from the degree of correctness and fullness of one's own contrition toward the freely given mercy of God (3.4.3, p. 626). He declares that Christ alone has established our peace with God once and for all (3.4.26–27, pp. 652–54). He wagers that this will correct two principal sinful consequences of the Roman methods: the "torture of souls...in a sea of trouble and anxiety" (3.4.1, p. 623) and "tyranny and superstition" (3.4.13, p. 638). The pattern of fixing upon the divine in order to address human problems repeats itself, as does his calibrating of the doctrine of sin to avoid both excessive optimism and despair. As usual he resorts to rhetorical hermeneutics to defend his position and to undermine the rival papal interpretations.

Calvin accuses his opponents of "butchery" by which souls seeking God are "cruelly torn." The "formulas" that "divided sins into arms, branches, twigs, and leaves" and then "weighed the qualities, quantities, and circumstances" only piled up a great inescapable mass of shame and thus left "no other outcome but despair." After creating these "wounds" the inept doctors offered pathetically inadequate remedies relying on the exertion of the penitent's feeble powers, so that new "terror" awaited (3.4.17, pp. 641–42).

Besides the needless suffering such dubious therapy occasioned, its efforts caused unchecked sin to become even more prevalent. Given our faulty memory, no human being could recall every transgression and so, by "depriving sinners of a true awareness of their sins, it makes them hypocrites" (3.4.18, p. 643) who put up a show of contrition to pass muster, since the standards of the reigning hamartiology could never be truly satisfied. Calvin detests the manner in which the people were "emboldened throughout the year to sin" and "heap up sins upon sins until they vomit all of them up at once." Calvin's critique of the distinction between mortal and venial sins similarly emerges from his concern that this subtlety will encourage persons to take sin lightly, whereas all opposition to God is deadly in consequence. It is no wonder, then, that he describes "auricular confession" as "a thing so pestilent and in so many ways harmful to the church!" (3.4.19, p. 645).

As the evidence presented in the last section would lead one to suspect, Calvin also discerns and opposes a will to power at work in what he considers a pseudo-sacrament. Since God bids us confess our sins before the divine throne (3.4.9, pp. 633–34), unburdening one's heart to another human being (not necessarily a minister, though a minister may be particularly competent) can be justified only on the basis of manifest practical utility. For instance, it may effect interpersonal reconciliation, encourage "mutual admonition and rebuke," or provide "relief" and "solace." Calvin's reasoning follows this rule: that "where God prescribes nothing definite, consciences be not bound with a definite yoke" (3.4.12, pp. 636–37). Therefore "we must always beware lest we dream up some power separate from the preaching of the gospel" (3.4.14, p. 639).

Yet in Calvin's eyes this is what the papacy has done. Consonant with his doctrine of the limits of human knowledge, Calvin realizes that no priest can be certain when faith and repentance are truly present (3.4.18, p. 644). When they nonetheless bind "the worthy and the unworthy indiscriminately, they usurp power without knowledge." The Word of judgment and promise alone enjoys that prerogative, but the clerics impudently cast it aside, for "they wished to rule lustfully, licentiously" (3.4.21, pp. 647–48) by making forgiveness depend solely upon their judgment (3.4.22, p. 648). Characteristically Calvin verbally blasts this unstable foundation as "an utterly intolerable sacrilege" (3.4.24, p. 650). And his campaign against the sacralization of priestly power also finds expression in his historical arguments seeking to persuade readers to reject the sacramental status of penance (4.19.14–17, pp. 1461–65). It is therefore also interesting to note that Calvin defends his position opposing the sacramental status of marriage by condemning the church's jurisdiction over domestic law as a "tyranny...most unfair toward men [sic]" (4.19.37, p. 1484).

So apparently prior to the appearance of the virtuosi of suspicion Christians could pursue hamartiology as a critique of oppressive doctrines of sin. Calvin's anger at psychological abusiveness is particularly striking. I therefore perceive an affinity between his work and the critical theorists whose rejections of the Christian teachings on human sinfulness I discussed earlier in this chapter. His analysis seeks to contribute to emancipation. Calvin knows that empowerment depends upon the achievement of a delicate balance. Unless persons understand how desperate their plight is, they will not seek alternatives. Yet if one overestimates the strength of evil, despair ensues, paralyzing people's ability to pursue necessary and possible changes. Calvin's consistent awareness of the ubiquity of sin permits him to see that the papal system has erred on both counts. And as always his solution demands complete reliance on a God who demands and enables persons to engage in active transformation of the human sphere of existence.

One should avoid overestimation of the affinities between past Christian polemic and critical discourse today. A rhetorical theory that prizes the principle of decorum will readily recognize the uniqueness of each historical context. Moreover, it would be anachronistic to suggest that the prophets or theologians I alluded to possessed critical theories in the contemporary sense. The tools of the social sciences had not been invented. And yet if we assume that the heart of a critical discourse is thorough analysis of a regime with the aim of loosening allegiance to it, it does not seem farfetched to postulate that the prophetic tradition of Christian hamartiology and contemporary emancipatory intellectual praxis share a common spirit. At the least I believe that I may safely claim that, to recall Lentricchia's criterion, hamartiology performed as rhetorical hermeneutics does have the potential of reading texts in ways that can inspire persons to actively address the horrors of our time.

The Catholicity and Historicity of Theology

In an article summarizing his own interpretation of John Calvin's theology, William Bouwsma offers systematic theologians
some advice. He postulates that our field is "a human activity
that is often remarkably sensitive to its historical context."[1] But
he charges that "the tendency of some theologians to think of theology as an activity that stands apart from other disciplines and
above them" has "subtly collaborated" with the "secularist bias"
of historians, that "tacit assumption that theology has little to
do with the real world" (29). In contrast he proposes that "an
understanding of the historicity of theological discourse may be
essential to a proper interpretation of its substance" (39).

And in this light Bouwsma finds Calvin continually instructive
precisely as a "historical artifact" (32). For this Reformer joined
the great controversies of his age and addressed himself to its particular problems. Bouwsma describes the humanism with which
Calvin readily identified his own work and which I have discussed
as a rhetorical enterprise in the Ciceronian tradition, as "a self-
conscious reform movement, concerned to reform not all times
but its own time." This sense of urgency led its partisans to reject "speculative system building" as a "luxury which the times
could ill afford. The times called for action!" (35). And like his
predecessors Calvin considered rhetoric the ideal instrument for
stimulating his contemporaries to vigorous transformative deeds.
He believed that God's Word was "all activity, power in action"
(36). Therefore Calvin sought to follow where it led. He employed
his considerable erudition not to increase the store of knowledge — all humans needed of that material was already available —
but to serve as a minister through whom God might overcome
the weakness and sluggishness of sin that prevented human beings
from performing those practical and useful tasks so vital to the

health of all. If Calvin's divine exemplar accommodated the unsurpassed glory first to the lowly nation of Israel and then to all human beings in the incarnation, how could the disciple do less than to consistently practice decorum, matching his message to fit the needs and capacities of his own unique moment in history?

I have dwelt on Bouwsma's article at length because it seems such a fitting summation of the case I have attempted to make in these pages. He presents Calvin as just one classical theologian who was willing to do his constructive work as a purely local, occasional, combative, and persuasive enterprise. Following the theological criterion of identity, the example of Calvin and many others not treated here demands that we consider the possibility that the essence of the Christian faith might reside in its willingness to follow the example of a God who, in the ongoing campaign to win joint respect for the divine honor and the sanctity of human lives, is willing to make constant strategic adjustments in ever-changing historical circumstances. I argue that both the relevance and the catholicity of theology as rhetorical hermeneutics reside in its ability to become a useful instrument for many different persons and groups in various locales and times. The brief illustration developed in my final chapter is one instance of the multiple uses to which a rhetorical methodology could be put.

Following Bouwsma's comments, I must stress that the fact that a method of rhetorical hermeneutics can be used by persons in different rhetorical situations commits its theological practitioners to the inescapable historicity of our discourse. We must be content to relinquish the goal of universal analyses, redefining catholicity as a rich pluralism of perspectives. While this mode of textual interpretation may derive inspiration from other contexts past and present, any particular theological reading takes place on a unique horizon, limiting itself to addressing a specific, unrepeatable audience and situation. In short, I am suggesting that theologians should be content if in retrospect their contribution becomes nothing more than an interesting historical artifact.

Some readers may worry that a theology thus making decorum its central methodological principle will tend to become all too provincial. But the historical study of personalities such as Calvin leads to the conclusion that every theology has been a local theology. Furthermore, those contributions that became the property of the whole church have been those that offered the unique gifts of their own particularity, asking the catholic community to consider their usefulness as such.[2]

Concerned persons may also fear the loss of transcendence or of the eschatological reserve, so that the present discourse becomes sacralized. The notorious case of the German Aryan Church remains as a stark reminder of this possibility. I have argued that the ethics of reverence for life functions as a transcendental and nonnegotiable ethical principle applicable in all situations. In spite of these safeguards, however, the recognition of the ubiquity of sin means that one can never rule out the risk of serious distortion. Rhetoric is ever in danger of falling into the trap of courting the audience so much that in the end the values of the hearers are not altered but reaffirmed.

But what are the alternatives? I critiqued antirhetorical epistemologies in chapter 3, noting that many contemporary critics of modernist universalism point to the oppressive effects of any epistemology pretending to be ahistorical. And can excessive hesitancy to act provide any better guarantee of a sin-free option? Given the overwhelming presence of unjust and avoidable death and degradation at the close of the twentieth century, might the risk of "unbalance," as Calvin once put it, not be worth taking? Shouldn't each person's anxious heart be reassured by a conviction that ultimately every sincere struggle will be acceptable and that God's preordained grace envelops the life of each pilgrim willing to embark on the journey toward God's kin-dom?[3]

As José Míguez Bonino has written:

A Christian has no self-image to preserve, no need to be justified by the blamelessness of his [sic] action, no value to attach to achievement beyond its significance for the neighbor, no claim to make on the basis of rightness. A Christian can offer his praxis to the fire of criticism totally and unreservedly on the trust of free grace just as he can offer his body totally and unreservedly in the hope of resurrection.... An eschatological faith makes it

possible for the Christian to invest his life historically
in the building of a temporary and imperfect order with
the certainty that neither he nor his effort is meaningless
or lost...confident...of the triumph of God's love and
solidarity.[4]

This work, then, represents an invitation to contemporary rhetorical theologies to gladly become artifacts, those objects of a
bygone, irrecoverable era that yet remain and dazzle succeeding
generations with the beauty of their odd singularity. For in this
particular time and place the existence of future admirers of archaeological findings may depend on it. Who would have thought
that acceptance of the fact that someday our labors will become
passé might become a profound affirmation of hope?

Notes

Preface

1. Francis Schüssler Fiorenza provides a helpful overview in "Systematic Theology: Task and Methods," in Francis Schüssler Fiorenza and John P. Galvin, eds., *Systematic Theology: Roman Catholic Perspectives* (Minneapolis: Fortress, 1991), 1–87. For just one example of the fact that the diversity is even greater than Fiorenza's treatment suggests, see Serene Jones, " 'Women's Experience' Between a Rock and a Hard Place: Feminist, Womanist and *Mujerista* Theologies in North America," *Religious Studies Review* 21 (July 1995): 171–78.

2. Perhaps Edward Farley's *Theologia: The Fragmentation and Unity of Theological Education* (Philadelphia: Fortress, 1983) has been particularly influential in this regard.

3. See, for instance, Rebecca Chopp, *Saving Work: Feminist Practices of Theological Education* (Louisville, Ky.: Westminster/John Knox, 1995).

4. David Tracy's analysis in *The Analogical Imagination: Christian Theology and the Culture of Pluralism* (New York: Crossroad, 1989) has touched off a significant debate about "public theology."

5. Cf. Stephen Sykes, *The Identity of Christianity: Theologians and the Essence of Christianity from Schleiermacher to Barth* (Philadelphia: Fortress, 1984).

6. Cf. Robert Schreiter, *Constructing Local Theologies* (Maryknoll, N.Y.: Orbis, 1985).

7. A point argued at length in the christological work of Edward Schillebeeckx. See *Jesus: An Experiment in Christology* (New York: Seabury, 1979) and *Christ: The Experience of Jesus as Lord* (New York: Crossroad, 1980). In a highly secularized country Schillebeeckx's work was widely read and awarded the Erasmus Prize in recognition of its contribution to Dutch culture.

1. An Introduction to the Rhetorical Tradition

1. *Gorgias*, trans. W. C. Hembold (Indianapolis: Bobbs-Merrill, 1952), par. 465 (p. 25).

2. *Phaedrus*, trans. W. C. Hembold and W. G. Rabinowitz (Indianapolis: Bobbs-Merrill, 1956). See also George A. Kennedy's discussion of these works in *Classical Rhetoric and Its Christian and Secular Tradition from Ancient to Modern Times* (Chapel Hill: University of North Carolina Press, 1980), 45–60; C. Jan Swearingen's creative interpretation in *Rhetoric and Irony: Western Literacy and Western Lies* (Oxford: Oxford University Press, 1991), 55–94;

and especially the spirited critical review in Brian Vickers, *In Defense of Rhetoric* (Oxford: Clarendon, 1988), 83–147.

3. (Notre Dame, Ind.: University of Notre Dame Press, 1969). The original French edition appeared in 1958.

4. *Plurality and Ambiguity: Hermeneutics, Religion, Hope* (San Francisco: Harper and Row, 1987), 122 n. 8.

5. (Notre Dame, Ind.: University of Notre Dame Press, 1990).

6. See Kennedy, *Classical Rhetoric*, 60, 81; and Victoria Kahn, *Rhetoric, Prudence, and Skepticism in the Renaissance* (Ithaca, N.Y.: Cornell University Press, 1985), 29, 199.

7. *De Oratore* 2.28, 3.35, in *Cicero on Oratory and Orators*, trans. or ed. J. S. Watson (Carbondale and Edwardsville: Southern Illinois University Press, 1970), 127, 232–33. See the discussion of Cicero's tactful caveats in Jerol Seigel, *Rhetoric and Philosophy in Renaissance Humanism: The Union of Eloquence and Wisdom, Petrarch to Valla* (Princeton, N.J.: Princeton University Press, 1968), 13–15.

8. The latest, and probably best, translation of this classic is that of George Kennedy, *Aristotle, On Rhetoric: A Theory of Civic Discourse* (Oxford: Oxford University Press, 1991). See 1.1.1354a (p. 30), and the change in tone as early as 1.2 (pp. 36–47). In his helpful introduction Kennedy suggests that such discontinuities may reflect the fact that the work that has come down to us was a collection of notes for lectures given at different times, or in any case a piece not in final shape for public distribution. If he is correct, I would suggest we have further reasons for not according definitive status to this treatise.

9. Cf. 1.2.1357a (p. 41): "Its [rhetoric's] function is concerned with the sort of things we debate . . . among such listeners as are not able to see many things all together or to reason from a distant starting point." But Aristotle doubts whether even oratory can move the masses to virtue: "while words evidently do have the power to encourage and stimulate young men of generous mind, and while they can cause a character well-born and truly enamored of what is noble to be possessed of virtue, they do not have the capacity to turn the common run of people to goodness and nobility . . . emotion does not yield to argument but only to force." *Nichomachean Ethics*, trans. Martin Ostwald (Indianapolis: Bobbs-Merrill, 1962), 10.9.1179b (pp. 295–96).

10. Seigel, *Rhetoric and Philosophy in Renaissance Humanism*, 15.

11. The essay by Donald C. Bryant, "Rhetoric: Its Function and Scope," *The Quarterly Journal of Speech* 39 (December 1953): 401–24, constitutes an instructive exception. His acceptance of Aristotle's restriction of rhetoric's scope and capacity rests on his charge that Cicero's standards for the ideal orator are "absurd" in "practice and in plausible human situations" (408), an accusation answered in my discussion of Cicero below.

12. In *Cicero: De Inventione. De Optimo Genere Oratorum. Topica*, The Loeb Classical Library, trans. H. M. Hubbell (Cambridge, Mass.: Harvard University Press, 1949), 1.5.6 (p. 15).

13. Here he is countering what he considers the baleful influence of Socrates.

14. In *Cicero: Brutus, Orator*, The Loeb Classical Library, trans. H. M. Hubbell (Cambridge, Mass.: Harvard University Press, 1962), 1.3–4 (p. 309) and the quotation from 2.7 (p. 311).

15. On this notion, which also becomes synonymous with culture, see Hans-Georg Gadamer's *Truth and Method*, trans. Garrett Barden and John Cumming (New York: Crossroad, 1988), 10–19.

16. Kennedy, *Classical Rhetoric*, 100–102.

17. For a brief statement of the requirements, see *De Oratore* 1.34 (p. 44).

18. Quoted in Seigel, *Rhetoric and Philosophy in Renaissance Humanism*, 142.

19. I refer to the translation by J. S. Watson, *Quintilian's Institutes of Oratory; Or, Education of an Orator*, 2 vols. (London: George Bell and Sons, 1875–76), 12.1.1 (vol. 2, p. 391), emphasis original.

20. For other versions of the material I will now summarize, see Vickers, *In Defense of Rhetoric*, 52–82; and Kenneth Burke, *A Rhetoric of Motives* (Berkeley: University of California Press, 1969), 49–78.

21. See the brief synopsis in *De Inventione* 1.5. (pp. 15–17).

22. See Kahn's discussion of the way the ethical notion of prudence became identified with the rhetorical principle of decorum in the Renaissance.

23. Obviously the subject of *De Inventione*.

24. Vickers, *In Defense of Rhetoric*, 294–339, also offers an effective defense against the charge of mere formalism.

25. Quintilian's treatment is far more extensive, covering much of books 8 and 9.

26. The popularity of the *Rhetorica ad Herennium*, long attributed to Cicero but now considered a work of a contemporary, rested in part on its unique mnemonic system in book 3, though the treatment of style in book 4 rivaled that of Quintilian. See the translation by Harry Caplan, The Loeb Classical Library (Cambridge, Mass.: Harvard University Press, 1964); and Kennedy, *Classical Rhetoric*, 96–99. For centuries this work and *De Inventione* served as the West's handbooks of classical rhetoric.

27. Bryant, "Rhetoric," 406–7. Cf. Burke, *Rhetoric of Motives*, 53–55.

28. See, for instance, the opening of *De Oratore* book 3 (pp. 192–94).

29. I refer to the translation by D. W. Robertson Jr. (New York: Macmillan, 1958).

30. David Tracy has recently made a good case for the rhetorical purpose and importance of the entirety of *De Doctrina Christiana* in "Charity, Obscurity, Clarity: Augustine's Search for Rhetoric and Hermeneutics," in *Rhetoric and Hermeneutics in Our Time*, ed. Walter Jost and Michael J. Hyde (New Haven, Conn.: Yale University Press, 1997), 254–74. Unfortunately he pays little attention to Book IV.

31. See James J. Murphy, *Rhetoric in the Middle Ages: A History of Rhe-*

torical Theory from St. Augustine to the Renaissance (Berkeley: University of California Press, 1974); and the works of Kahn and Seigel. I also recommend the helpful summary by William J. Bouwsma, "The Spirituality of Renaissance Humanism," in *Christian Spirituality: High Middle Ages and Reformation*, ed. Jill Raitt (New York: Crossroad, 1996), 236–51.

32. Knut Alfsvag, "Language and Reality: Luther's Relation to Classical Rhetoric in *Rationis Latomianae Confutatio* (1521)," *Studia Theologica* 41 (1987): 85–126.

33. Ford Lewis Battles, "God Was Accommodating Himself to Human Capacity," *Interpretation* 31 (1977): 19–38. The most thorough study of Calvin's rhetoric to date is Olivier Millet's *Calvin et la dynamique de la parole: Etude de rhétorique réformée* (Paris: Librairie Honoré Champion, 1992).

34. I refer to Newman's *An Essay in Aid of a Grammar of Assent* (1870; New York: Doubleday, 1955). See Walter Jost, *Rhetorical Thought in John Henry Newman* (Columbia: University of South Carolina, 1989).

35. Cf. Wayne C. Booth, "Rhetoric and Religion: Are They Essentially Wedded?" in *Radical Pluralism and Truth: David Tracy and the Hermeneutics of Religion*, ed. Werner G. Jeanrond and Jennifer L. Rike (New York: Crossroad, 1991), 62–79.

36. See Walter J. Ong, S.J., *Ramus, Method and the Decay of Dialogue* (Cambridge, Mass.: Harvard University Press, 1958).

37. *Discourse on Method and Meditations*, trans. Lawrence J. Lafleur (Indianapolis: Bobbs-Merrill, 1960), 7–8. I have benefited from the analysis of Descartes by Richard Rorty, *Philosophy and the Mirror of Nature* (Princeton, N.J.: Princeton University Press, 1979).

38. "The Reader in History: The Changing Shape of Literary Response," in *Reader-Response Criticism: From Formalism to Post-Structuralism*, ed. Jane Tompkins (Baltimore and London: Johns Hopkins University Press, 1980), 201–32. I have also benefited from Terry Eagleton's *Literary Theory: An Introduction* (Minneapolis: University of Minnesota Press, 1983), which weaves a similar tale.

39. Marshall McLuhan and Walter J. Ong have also made much of the way printing undermined rhetorical culture. See McLuhan's *The Gutenberg Galaxy* (Toronto: University of Toronto Press, 1962) and Ong's *Rhetoric, Romance, and Technology* (Ithaca, N.Y.: Cornell University Press, 1971).

40. Cf. Thomas Heller: "The claim to a meta-status for theory may be seen as a claim to institutional power for the practitioners of the theory." Quoted in Stanley Fish, "Introduction: Going Down the Anti-Formalist Road," in his *Doing What Comes Naturally: Change, Rhetoric, and the Practice of Theory in Literary and Legal Studies* (Durham, N.C.: Duke University Press, 1989), 25.

41. See also Steven Mailloux's discussion of the New Criticism and reader-response criticism in *Rhetorical Power* (Ithaca, N.Y., and London: Cornell University Press, 1989), 19–53.

42. In even sharper terms Mailloux (51–52) alleges that "reader criticism tended to ignore the ideological debates of a wider cultural politics extending beyond the academy, and insofar as most reader-response approaches avoided the issues of race, class, and gender, for example, they supported conservative voices that attempted to cordon off the university in general and literary criticism in particular from directly engaging in any kind of radical politics."

2. Theology as Rhetorical Hermeneutics

1. A vast literature exists that contests the meaning(s) of this catch-all term. A good starting place is provided by Jean-François Lyotard, *The Post-modern Condition: A Report on Knowledge*, trans. Geoff Bennington and Brian Massumi (Minneapolis: University of Minnesota Press, 1984). One of the more penetrating critical gazes turned on postmodernity has been that of Jürgen Habermas, *The Philosophical Discourses of Modernity: Twelve Lectures*, trans. Frederick G. Lawrence (Cambridge, Mass.: MIT Press, 1990).

2. *Friedrich Nietzsche on Rhetoric and Language*, ed. and trans. Sander L. Gilman, Carole Blair, and David J. Parent (New York: Oxford University Press, 1989). See the discussion of Nietzsche in Habermas, *Philosophical Discourses of Modernity*, 83–105. Nietzsche's influence on all postmodern writers cannot be overestimated. One clear indication of his centrality is provided by David B. Allison, ed., *The New Nietzsche: Contemporary Styles of Interpretation* (New York: Delta, 1997), which includes essays by luminaries such as Jacques Derrida, Maurice Blanchot, and Gilles Deleuze.

3. Kuhn, 2d ed. (Chicago: University of Chicago Press, 1970). The impact of Einstein's theory of relativity, quantum physics, and other factors may have been decisive as well, since it would appear that the rise of modern science was initially linked to the Newtonian universe. On oratory's growing influence, see, for instance, R. H. Roberts and J. M. M. Good, eds., *The Recovery of Rhetoric: Persuasive Discourse and Disciplinarity in the Human Sciences* (Charlottesville: University of Virginia Press, 1993). The German series *Rhetorik*, "Ein internationales Jahrbuch" (Stuttgart: Fromman-Holzboog, 1980–) demonstrates the international character of this movement.

4. For a helpful overview and extensive bibliography, consult Duane F. Watson and Alan J. Hauser, *Rhetorical Criticism and the Bible: A Comprehensive Bibliography with Notes on History and Method* (Leiden: E. J. Brill, 1994).

5. See, for instance, Gert Ott, *Predigt als rhetorische Aufgabe: homiletische Perspektiven* (Neukirchen-Vluyn: Neukirchener Verlag, 1987). Many useful articles appear in *The Journal of Communication and Religion*, published by the Religious Speech Communication Association.

6. Alain Le Boulluec's work, *La notion de l'hérésie dans la littérature grecque Ile–IIIe siècles*, 2 vols. (Paris: Études Augustiniennes, 1985), should soon be further refined by the forthcoming studies of J. Rebecca Lyman.

7. For a succinct overview, see Rebecca S. Chopp, *The Praxis of Suffer-*

ing: An Interpretation of Liberation and Political Theologies (Maryknoll, N.Y.: Orbis, 1986), 29–33. Cf. her *The Power to Speak: Feminism, Language, God* (New York: Crossroad, 1989), 5: "Protestant theology, at least as defined by modern revisionist schools, both liberal and neoorthodox, worries over its own lack of relevance." As she suggests in footnote 17 on page 132, this judgment does not apply to liberation theologies. It seems that two competing definitions of publicness underlie this difference; see my comments concerning evangelization and *diakonia* below.

8. Gareth Jones, *Critical Theology: Questions of Truth and Method* (New York: Paragon House, 1995), 204. He cites no theological literature in support of this sweeping claim.

9. See Eberhard Busch, *Karl Barth: His Life from Letters and Autobiographical Texts* (Philadelphia: Fortress, 1976).

10. Metz, *Faith in History and Society: Toward a Fundamental Practical Theology*, trans. David Smith (New York: Seabury, 1980), and Browning, *A Fundamental Practical Theology: Descriptive and Strategic Proposals* (Minneapolis: Fortress, 1991). Cf. the frequent references to Barth's work in Gustavo Gutiérrez's *On Job: God-Talk and the Suffering of the Innocent*, trans. Matthew J. O'Connell (Maryknoll, N.Y.: Orbis, 1987).

11. Two of my favorite examples would be Robert McAfee Brown and Justo González. See, for instance, Brown's *Gustavo Gutiérrez* (Atlanta: John Knox, 1980) and González's *Mañana: Christian Theology from a Hispanic Perspective* (Nashville: Abingdon, 1990).

12. Compare Clodovis Boff's *Theology and Praxis: Epistemological Foundations*, trans. Robert R. Barr (Maryknoll, N.Y.: Orbis, 1987) with Ada María Isasi-Díaz and Yolanda Tarango, *Hispanic Women: Prophetic Voice in the Church* (San Francisco: Harper and Row, 1988). I am grateful to Professor Isasi-Díaz for her oral explication of this point during the Summer Hispanic Program of the Fund for Theological Education, Chicago, June 1991.

13. *The Nature of Doctrine: Religion and Theology in a Postliberal Age* (Philadelphia: Westminster, 1984).

14. Schreiter, *Constructing Local Theologies* (Maryknoll, N.Y.: Orbis, 1985), and Shorter, *Toward a Theology of Inculturation* (Maryknoll, N.Y.: Orbis, 1988).

15. Mark C. Taylor's works, such as *Erring: A Postmodern A/theology* (Chicago: University of Chicago Press, 1984), are perhaps the best known but by no means the only instances of this trend. I will return to this theme in considerable more detail in the next chapter.

16. While I cannot agree with all aspects of Taylor's portrayal of the melancholy Dane, the promotion of contingency in the *Concluding Unscientific Postscript*, trans. David F. Swenson and Walter Lowrie (Princeton, N.J.: Princeton University Press, 1941) seems undeniable — and, incidentally, demonstrates that this worldview need not entail relativism. I am grateful to Professors Walter Lowe and Don Saliers for many discussions about "SK."

Kierkegaard would provide further corroboration for the link between sin and epistemology developed in chapter 3.

17. Míguez Bonino, *Doing Theology in a Revolutionary Situation* (Philadelphia: Fortress, 1975); Cone, *A Black Theology of Liberation* (Philadelphia and New York: J. B. Lippincott, 1970); and Schüssler Fiorenza, *In Memory of Her: A Feminist Theological Reconstruction of Christian Origins* (New York: Crossroad, 1983).

18. In addition to *Theologia*, see *The Fragility of Knowledge: Theological Education in the Church and the University* (Philadelphia: Fortress, 1988).

19. See especially his *Christmas Eve: Dialogue on the Incarnation*, trans. Terrence N. Tice (Richmond, Va.: John Knox, 1967). For an overview of the renewed consideration of Schleiermacher's theology, see James O. Duke and Robert F. Streetman, eds., *Barth and Schleiermacher: Beyond the Impasse?* (Philadelphia: Fortress, 1988).

20. Jones's interesting work offers a telling example. He devotes an entire chapter to rhetoric, but without any reference to Aristotle, Cicero, or Augustine. Thus the term becomes a generic synonym for "communication." And he insists that rhetoric has no place in the act of interpretation itself, thus setting himself at odds with the persuasive practice of the Roman tradition of rhetorical hermeneutics.

21. David Tracy, *The Analogical Imagination: Christian Theology and the Culture of Pluralism* (New York: Crossroad, 1989), 155.

22. See *Plurality and Ambiguity: Hermeneutics, Religion, and Hope* (San Francisco: Harper and Row, 1987), 113–14 and footnote 72 on 142. In *The Analogical Imagination*, 163, he says: "Unlike the classics of art, morality, science and politics, explicitly religious classics will involve a claim to truth as the event of a disclosure-concealment of the whole of reality *by the power of the whole* — as, in some sense, a radical and finally gracious mystery" (emphasis original).

23. *Plurality and Ambiguity*, 107. The indictment of elitism appears on 102–5. The complexity of Tracy's argumentation, syntax, and so forth can smack of elitism until one realizes that he is probably adapting his speech to the requirements of a particular scholarly audience. This is suggested by Tracy's own analysis of the three publics of theology — academy, church, and society — in *The Analogical Imagination*, 3–31.

24. *Plurality and Ambiguity*, 103–4 and footnote 56 on 141.

25. Cf. this distinction drawn by Míguez Bonino: "This [i.e., Latin American] theology finds its place in the history of theology in the range of what could be called the *theologies of salvation* as different from 'theologies of revelation.' That is, it is more interested in questions of life than in questions of meaning. Its main question is how can the Christian faith transform human life and situations rather than how can it give meaning to or clarify the meaning of life. Again, it hardly needs saying that transformation demands clarification, that revelation and redemption cannot be separated. But

we are dealing here with an order of priority, not with a reduction of one discourse to another." "Theology as Critical Reflection and Liberating Praxis," in *The Vocation of the Theologian*, ed. Theodore W. Jennings Jr. (Philadelphia: Fortress, 1985), 38.

26. "New Trends in Theology," *Duke Divinity School Review* 42 (1977): 137. I am grateful for personal discussions with Professor Míguez on this subject.

27. In addition to works already cited, I anticipate the publication next year of a volume entitled *Rhetoric and Religion in Our Time*, with essays by significant theologians such as Tracy and Stanley Hauerwas.

28. *Re-figuring Theology: The Rhetoric of Karl Barth* (Albany: State University of New York Press, 1991); *Blessed Excess: Religion and the Hyperbolic Imagination* (Albany: State University of New York Press, 1993); and *The Gifting God: A Trinitarian Ethics of Excess* (New York: Oxford University Press, 1996). I am grateful to Professor Webb for his perceptive critique of an earlier draft of this work.

29. Wayne C. Booth considers the promotion of plural voices another strong argument in favor of rhetorical approaches ("Rhetoric and Religion: Are They Essentially Wedded?" in *Radical Pluralism and Truth: David Tracy and the Hermeneutics of Religion*, ed. Werner G. Jeanrond and Jennifer L. Rike [New York: Crossroad, 1991], 79–80).

30. *The Gifting God*, v–vi. See also his *On God and Dogs: A Christian Theology of Compassion for Animals* (New York: Oxford University Press, 1998).

31. I was grateful for the opportunity to read the draft of David's second major work, *These Three Are One: The Practice of Trinitarian Theology* (Oxford: Blackwell Publishers, 1998). Since I know him personally, I should also hasten to add that his actions (opposition to the Gulf War, for instance) demonstrate that praxis is of far more concern to him than his first book suggests.

32. As our conversations have taught me, David rejects them for the right ethical reasons: Cicero represented the elite class of Roman landowners, and Quintilian worked for a despotic emperor. But much the same could be said of Aristotle, tutor of Alexander the Great.

33. And the Anglican tradition both of us represent. Long ago H. R. McAdoo pointed to the "occasional" character of English moral discourse in the seventeenth century; see *The Structure of Caroline Moral Theology* (London: Longmans, Green, 1949). Richard Hooker is now often considered the theological founder of this tradition, and both William J. Bouwsma and I, among others, have detected the unmistakable evidence of rhetorical training in the writings of this divine; consult Bouwsma's "Hooker in the Context of European Cultural History" and my "Hooker on the Authority of Scripture in Matters of Morality" in *The Interpreted Establishment: Richard Hooker and the Construction of Christian Community*, ed. A. S. McGrade (Tempe, Ariz.: Medieval and Renaissance Texts and Studies, 1997), 65–84; 314–25.

34. "El conocimiento teológico en la teología europea y latinoamericana," in *Liberación y cautiverio: Debates en torno al método de la teología en América Latina*, ed. Enrique Ruíz Maldonado (Mexico City: Encuentro Latinoamericano de Teología, 1975), 177–207 (quote from 206). For a similar discussion, see Gustavo Gutiérrez, *La fuerza histórica de los pobres* (Salamanca: Ediciones Sígueme, 1982), 215–76; ET "Theology from the Underside of History," in *The Power of the Poor in History: Selected Writings*, trans. Robert R. Barr (Maryknoll, N.Y.: Orbis, 1983).

35. See also an earlier essay, "Theological Persuasion: Rhetoric, Warrants, and Suffering," in *Worldview and Warrants: Plurality and Ambiguity in Theology*, ed. William Schweiker and Per M. Anderson (Lanham, Md.: University Press of America, 1987), 17–31. Rhetorical insights are applied to theological education in her most recent book, *Saving Work: Feminist Practices of Theological Education* (Louisville, Ky.: Westminster/John Knox, 1995), especially 91–93.

36. Chopp has used the phrase employed by Gaetra Spivak and others to speak of theology as the exercise of cultural politics. See, for instance, "From Patriarchy into Freedom: A Conversation Between American Feminist Theology and French Feminism," in *Transfigurations: Theology and the French Feminists*, ed. C. W. Maggie Kim, Susan M. St. Ville, and Susan M. Simonaitis (Minneapolis: Fortress, 1993), 31–48.

37. I am convinced that the political effectiveness of theology will depend on the recovery of the type of publicness practiced by McAfee Brown and González. But the density of Professor Chopp's text once again (and understandably) reflects the nature of the academic audience she was addressing.

38. Schüssler Fiorenza has offered a particularly evocative statement of her feminist approach to history in "The 'Quilting' of Women's History: Phoebe of Cenchreae," in *Embodied Love: Sensuality and Relationship as Feminist Values*, ed. Paula M. Cooey, Sharon A. Farmer, and Mary Ellen Ross (San Francisco: Harper and Row, 1987), 35–49.

39. So has Bradford T. Stull in *Religious Dialectics of Pain and Imagination* (Albany: State University of New York, 1994), but as he freely admits, he makes rather limited use of the rhetorical traditions and devotes the bulk of his book to an interpretation of Kenneth Burke, Thomas Merton, Paulo Freire, and Oscar Romero.

40. See her "Feminism's Theological Pragmatics: A Social Naturalism of Women's Experience," *Journal of Religion* 67 (April 1987): 239–56. A forthcoming book she is cowriting with Michael Wyatt will develop pragmatism's contribution to theology at greater length.

41. Along with Terry Eagleton, it is helpful to be able to say that like "all the best radical positions, mine is a thoroughly traditional one" (*Literary Theory: An Introduction* [Minneapolis: University of Minnesota Press, 1983], 206).

42. Cf. William Dean, *The Religious Critic in American Culture* (Albany:

State University of New York Press, 1994), and Cornel West, *The American Evasion of Philosophy: A Genealogy of Pragmatism* (Madison: University of Wisconsin Press, 1989).

43. *Criticism and Social Change* (Chicago: University of Chicago, 1983), 10, 12. Much of this work is devoted to a reading of Kenneth Burke, one of the pioneers of the revival of rhetorical hermeneutics.

44. See, for instance, Míguez Bonino, *Doing Theology in a Revolutionary Situation*, 119–20: "If class struggle is a fact...then a love which intends to be effective in terms of God's Kingdom cannot avoid taking sides."

45. "Introduction: Going Down the Anti-Formalist Road," in Fish's *Doing What Comes Naturally: Change, Rhetoric and the Practice of Theory in Literary and Legal Studies* (Durham, N.C.: Duke University Press, 1989), 7.

46. In Jones's lovely phrase, "rhetoric in theology functions as the dangerous science of the possible, for the sake of the inexpressible, in the hands of the hopeful" (*Critical Theology*, 109).

3. Rhetorical Epistemology

1. *Theology and Praxis: Epistemological Foundations*, trans. Robert R. Barr (Maryknoll, N.Y.: Orbis, 1987), xxix. While when they mention rhetoric Latin American liberation theologians almost always refer to it in the pejorative sense of "mere rhetoric." I believe Gareth Jones correctly analyzes Jon Sobrino's theology as in effect a rhetorical performance (*Critical Theology: Questions of Truth and Method* [New York: Paragon House, 1995], 85–112).

2. I borrow these terms from Richard Bernstein's *Beyond Objectivism and Relativism: Science, Hermeneutics, and Praxis* (Philadelphia: University of Pennsylvania Press, 1988), a helpful entree into the complex epistemological debates of our time.

3. "Theological Persuasion: Rhetoric, Warrants, and Suffering," in *Worldview and Warrants: Plurality and Ambiguity in Theology*, ed. William Schweiker and Per M. Anderson (Lanham, Md.: University Press of America, 1987), 19.

4. Referring to Stanley Fish's *Is There a Text in This Class? The Authority of Interpretive Communities* (Cambridge, Mass.: Harvard University Press, 1980).

5. Cf. Mailloux's concluding section on the interpretive disputes surrounding the ABM treaties (170–81). While radically different construals of the meaning of those documents are discussed, none of the debaters claims that the text has been incorrectly transmitted, nor can the debaters claim that given words appear in a place where in fact they do not.

6. Notably Fish and Bernstein. The former rests his case on the power of whatever convictions reign at present, while the latter trusts that communities committed to serious ongoing dialogue offer the best human hope for practical truth serving the common interest. While committed to conversations, the rhetorical viewpoint presented here considers even Bernstein's

nuanced view too naive, for reasons emerging from the consideration of the epistemological effects of sin (see below). Thus I have serious reservations about the way in which the influence of Wittgenstein and like-minded scholars has also given credence in theological circles to what Peter Berger and Thomas Luckmann called *The Social Construction of Reality* (New York: Doubleday, 1966); in this regard George Lindbeck's influential work is particularly worthy of note.

7. Dean's work represents a solid analysis of the operation of social conventions.

8. Fish's contribution, which echoes in the work of theologians such as Stanley Hauerwas.

9. See the overview in Fish's "rhetoric," in *Doing What Comes Naturally: Change, Rhetoric, and the Practice of Theory in Literary and Legal Studies* (Durham, N.C.: Duke University Press, 1989), 471–502, though he evinces a rather dismissive attitude toward those whom, in Richard Lanham's terms, believe "we are members of the species *homo seriosus*" rather than that of *homo rhetoricus* (482). I find the terminology of this dichotomy singularly unfortunate; in my view rhetoric can be serious business indeed.

10. Cf. G. E. Lessing's famous dictum: "The worth of a man [sic] does not consist in the truth he possesses...but in the pains he has taken to attain that truth....In this alone his ever growing perfection consists. Possession makes him lazy, indolent, and proud. If God held all truth in his [sic] right hand and in his left the everlasting striving after truth, so that I should always and everlastingly be mistaken, and said to me, 'Choose,' with humility I would pick on the left hand and say 'Father, grant me that. Absolute truth is for thee alone.'" From the *Rejoinder* of 1778, quoted in Henry Chadwick, ed. and trans., *Lessing's Theological Writings* (Palo Alto, Calif.: Stanford University Press, 1956), 42–43. This quote suggests that recognition of the limitations of human knowledge does not excuse one from the need and duty to seek after the truth. Nihilism assumes that ultimately truth represents a chimerical holy grail; classical rhetoric does not share this pessimistic conviction.

11. Recently filmmaker Tim Robbins made this case with great eloquence in the movie *Dead Man Walking*. Schweitzer offers a succinct statement of his ethical philosophy in his essay on "The Ethics of Reverence for Life," included in Henry Clark's *The Ethical Mysticism of Albert Schweitzer: A Study of the Sources and Significance of Schweitzer's Philosophy of Civilization* (Boston: Beacon, 1962), 180–94. For a much fuller development of this theme, see Kathryn Tanner, *The Politics of God: Christian Theologies and Social Justice* (Minneapolis: Fortress, 1992).

12. I speak here out of my own context but maintain that much the same could be said of Muslims, Jews, and persons from other faith traditions with which I am less familiar. I also realize that many relativists do not relativize the priority of human lives. I find Foucault's thought particularly instructive

on this point and therefore must disagree with aspects of Welch's depiction of his work (more below).

13. In regard to feminist debates on these issues, see Diana Fuss's suggestive *Essentially Speaking: Feminism, Nature and Difference* (New York and London: Routledge, 1989).

14. Brian Vickers provides a useful discussion of figures, often overlooked as "mere ornamentation" (*In Defense of Rhetoric* [Oxford: Clarendon, 1988], 294–339).

15. Without thereby for a moment denying the social nature of the human species.

16. *Communities of Resistance and Solidarity: A Feminist Theology of Liberation* (Maryknoll, N.Y.: Orbis, 1985) and *A Feminist Ethic of Risk* (Minneapolis: Fortress, 1990). Cornel West wrote a perceptive review of the first book, "On Sharon D. Welch's *Communities of Resistance and Solidarity*," in his *Prophetic Fragments* (Grand Rapids, Mich.: Eerdmans; Trenton, N.J.: Africa World Press, 1988), 207–11.

17. Cf. the odd dichotomy on 86, when Welch "emphasizes that faith is not primarily declarative but revolutionary."

18. Cf. David Jasper, *Rhetoric, Power and Community* (Louisville, Ky.: Westminster/John Knox, 1993), which demonstrates the same hermeneutic of suspicion toward any use of rhetoric other than the constant employment of irony.

19. For a thorough critique of incommensurability theses, see Wayne C. Booth, *Modern Dogma and the Rhetoric of Assent* (Chicago: University of Chicago Press, 1974) and *Now Don't Try to Reason with Me: Essays and Ironies for a Credulous Age* (Chicago: University of Chicago Press, 1970). Iris Marion Young, a theorist committed to the recognition of radical pluralism, still eschews total incommensurability: "Difference ... is not absolute otherness, a complete absence of relationship or shared attributes ... subjects are not opaque to one another"; *Justice and the Politics of Difference* (Princeton, N.J.: Princeton University Press, 1990), 98, 105.

20. A tendency that becomes particularly evident in the third part of *A Feminist Ethic of Risk*, 103–80.

21. In the second book (p. 9, for instance) this theme undergoes a certain modification, so that Welch refuses to accept the inevitability of the triumph of the antinuclear forces but also insists that atomic holocaust is no foregone conclusion either. But her theoretical presuppositions remain the same, and I am suggesting in this section that a certain pessimism is the inevitable corollary of belief in discursive incommensurability.

22. Cf. West, *Prophetic Fragments*, 210.

23. In his debate with Noam Chomsky on Dutch television Foucault was driven to precisely this conclusion. Dismissing the notion of a just war, he said that the "proletariat makes war with the ruling class because ... it wants to take power.... One makes war to win, not because it is just.... When the

proletariat takes power, it may be quite possible that the proletariat will exert toward the classes over which it has just triumphed, a violent, dictatorial and even bloody power. I can't see what objection one could make to this." "Human Nature: Justice versus Power," in *Reflexive Waters: The Basic Concerns of Mankind*, ed. Fons Elders (London: Souvenir Press, 1974), 182. Two caveats: As I indicate below, I believe that other passages in Foucault's corpus affirm rhetorical routes to social change; and I don't mean to suggest that violent resistance is never justifiable but only that an ethic of reverence for life requires exhausting every other alternative first. Cf. my comments on Aristotle in footnote 9 of chapter 1.

24. In a future book I intend to offer an extensive rhetorical and theological interpretation of Foucault's work.

25. As her source for this statement Welch refers to Foucault's *The Archaeology of Knowledge*, trans. Alan Sheridan (New York: Pantheon, 1972), written in 1969.

26. Cf. Hubert L. Dreyfus and Paul Rabinow, *Michel Foucault: Beyond Structuralism and Hermeneutics*, 2d ed. (Chicago: University of Chicago Press, 1983), 132–33, 165–66.

27. *The Order of Things: An Archaeology of the Human Sciences* (New York: Vintage, 1973); *Power/Knowledge: Selected Interviews and Other Writings, 1972–1977*, ed. Colin Gordon (New York: Pantheon, 1980); and *The History of Sexuality*, vol. 1, *An Introduction*, trans. Robert Hurley (New York: Vintage, 1980).

28. *Michel Foucault's Force of Flight: Toward an Ethics for Thought* (Atlantic Highlands, N.J.: Humanities Press, 1990).

29. "Power and Strategies," trans. Colin Gordon, in *Power/Knowledge*, 134–45.

30. *Discipline and Punishment: The Birth of the Prison*, trans. Alan Sheridan (New York: Vintage, 1979), 30.

31. "What Is Enlightenment?" (1984, the year of his death), trans. Catherine Porter, in *The Foucault Reader*, ed. Paul Rabinow (New York: Pantheon, 1984), 32–50.

32. Thomas Flynn writes that the "result [of Foucault's work] is not epistemic anarchy. The proliferation of events and truths in Foucault's discourse is not without rhyme or reason"; "Foucault as Parrhesiast," in *The Final Foucault*, ed. James Bernauer and David Rasmussen (Cambridge, Mass.: MIT Press, 1988), 113. See also his defense of Foucault against the critiques leveled by Habermas in "Foucault and the Politics of Postmodernity," *Nous* 23 (April 1989): 187–98, summarized nicely on 192: "Foucault, who counsels limited resistances, is also satisfied with limited 'reasons'. As Rorty insists, 'if one is willing, as Dewey and Foucault were, to give up hope of universalism, then one can give up the fear of relativism as well.'" That is what I advocate in this chapter by arguing that limited reasons are reasonable just the same. I am grateful to Professor Flynn for guiding my explorations in Foucault's thought.

33. Cf. his wonder at the outbreak of mass popular resistance during the Iranian revolution; "Iran: The Spirit of a World Without Spirit," interview with Claire Briere and Pierre Blanchet, in *Michel Foucault: Politics, Philosophy, Culture. Interviews and Other Writings, 1977–1984,* ed. Lawrence D. Kritzman (New York and London: Routledge, 1988), 211–24.

34. See Flynn's "Michel Foucault and the Career of the Historical Event," in *At the Nexus of Philosophy and History,* ed. Bernard P. Dauenhauer (Athens and London: University of Georgia Press, 1987), 178–200; and "Foucault and Historical Nominalism," in *Phenomenology and Beyond: The Self and Its Language,* ed. H. A. Durfee and D. F. T. Rodier (Leiden: Kluwer Academic Publishers, 1989), 134–47.

35. *The History of Sexuality,* vol. 2, *The Use of Pleasure,* trans. Robert Hurley (New York: Vintage, 1985), 8–9, compared with the original, *Histoire de la sexualité 2: L'usage des plaisirs* (Paris: Gallimard, 1984), 14–15. In a fitting tribute, Gilles Deleuze read this passage at Foucault's funeral.

36. Mailloux repeatedly refers to Foucault.

37. In addition to *The Use of Pleasure,* see *The History of Sexuality,* vol. 3, *The Care of the Self,* trans. Robert Hurley (New York: Vintage, 1986), and the interview included in Dreyfus and Rabinow, 229–52, "On the Genealogy of Ethics: An Overview of Work in Progress." For theologians it is particularly unfortunate that his untimely death left his reflections on patristic sources forever unfinished, for the reports emerging from his final lectures are tantalizing. See Patrick Vandermeersch, "Michel Foucault: een onverwachte hermeneutiek van het christendom?" *Tijdschrift voor Theologie* 25 (1985): 250–77.

38. *Discipline and Punishment,* 31. He says he does not write about the emergence of prisons and the like "simply because I am interested in the past."

39. See *Communities of Resistance and Solidarity,* 25, 32, and elsewhere.

40. To cite just one instance, she lumps Karl Barth's transcendent theism and that of Paul Tillich under the same category of "valorization of absolute power" (*A Feminist Ethics of Risk,* 116–22), apparently failing to realize that the quotes from Tillich she employs are at times almost paraphrases of Hegel's *Philosophy of Right,* which probably represents a stoic worldview as much as or more than a Christian one; cf. the edition edited and translated by T. M. Knox (Oxford: Clarendon, 1952). In this section she also neglects to consider the counterbalance to utter transcendence that the Christian doctrine of the incarnation always provided. See, for instance, Justo González, *Mañana: Christian Theology from a Hispanic Perspective* (Nashville: Abingdon, 1990), 101–15.

41. Particularly in her reflections on the character of Harriet in Paule Marshall's novel *The Chosen Place, the Timeless People,* in *A Feminist Ethics of Risk,* 49–64.

42. I hope it is not necessary to state that nothing I have said in this

friendly critique of Welch should be interpreted as antifeminist polemic. In *Beyond Oppression: Feminist Theory and Political Strategy* (New York: Continuum, 1990, 110–29) Susan Hawkesworth has provided an overview of various different rhetorical strategies deployed by various feminist writers in their struggles against sexism. Theories of communicative incommensurability are by no means characteristic of feminist theories as a whole, as Fuss also contends. To use an "agonistic" analogy (Burke), my differences with Welch are tactical, not strategic.

43. *Theology and Praxis*, 236. In Aristotle's schema "general principles" are used in dialectic, of which rhetoric forms a subtype (*On Rhetoric* 1354a, p. 29).

44. See *Aristotle: Selections*, ed. W. D. Ross (New York: Scribners, 1927), 35–38. But as a good Thomist Boff must of course qualify his views in light of Aquinas's remarks about the analogical nature of theological language that persists in spite of the noetic superiority of revealed data.

45. Hence Immanuel Kant distinguished between an analytic sentence, in which the predicate is already contained in the definition of the subject, and a synthetic statement, in which the predicate adds information (akin to Aristotle's "accidents") not by necessity inherent in the substance of the subject. See *Prologomena to Any Future Metaphysic*, ed. Lewis White Beck (Indianapolis: Bobbs-Merrill, 1950), 14–15. But unlike his predecessor Leibniz, Kant wants to argue for the validity of experience-based synthetic judgments. I am grateful to Professor Walter Lowe for guiding my study of Kant's philosophy.

46. René Descartes's famous *Discourse on Method* was designed to perform precisely this "service."

47. Citing Louis Althusser.

48. On 290 Boff cites only Wittgenstein's *Tractatus Logico-Philosophicus*, but the sociological theorists with whom he is in dialogue also reflect the influence of the *Philosophical Investigations*, 3d ed., trans. G. E. M. Anscombe (New York: Macmillan, 1953), in which Wittgenstein elaborated his nonanalytical theory of language. I am grateful to a conversation with Professor Míguez Bonino in November 1991 in which he described the critiques Boff received at meetings of Latin American theologians, leading him to revise his earlier epistemological views. I also thank Professor Don Saliers for guiding my study of Wittgenstein's linguistic theory.

49. See, for instance, *Feet-on-the-Ground Theology: A Brazilian Journey*, trans. Phillip Berryman (Maryknoll, N.Y.: Orbis, 1987). From a rhetorical perspective one would have to note how his audience has changed. He says that he now writes "primarily for lay pastoral ministers, or activists among the poor" (xi).

50. See the introduction to *The Concept of Anxiety*, trans. Reidar Thomte and Albert B. Anderson (Princeton, N.J.: Princeton University Press, 1980), especially 9–10, 12. In the *Concluding Unscientific Postscript* he submits the objectivity of Hegelian philosophy to a series of epistemological and ethical critiques.

51. From lectures entitled "Description of Ancient Rhetoric" (1873), in *Friedrich Nietzsche on Rhetoric and Language*, ed. Sander L. Gilman, Carole Blair, and David J. Parent, 20–23.

52. Etymology continues to provide a methodological resource in Nietzsche's later work. See *On the Genealogy of Morals*, trans. Walter Kaufmann and R. J. Hollingdale, in a single volume with *Ecce Homo* (New York: Vintage, 1969).

53. From "On Truth and Lying in an Extra-Moral Sense," in *Friedrich Nietzsche on Language and Rhetoric*, ed. Gilman, Blair, and Parent, 246–57.

54. See part 1, "On the Prejudices of Philosophers," in *Beyond Good and Evil*, trans. Walter Kaufmann (New York: Vintage, 1966), 9–32.

55. The quote refers to the title of one of Nietzsche's works, excerpted in *The Portable Nietzsche*, ed. and trans. Walter J. Kaufmann (New York: Viking, 1954), 51–64.

56. See especially Richard Rorty's depiction of the metaphorical basis of Cartesianism and modern empiricism in *Philosophy and the Mirror of Nature* (Princeton, N.J.: Princeton University Press, 1979), and the broader reflections of Jacques Derrida, notably in "White Mythology: Metaphor in the Text of Philosophy," in *Margins of Philosophy*, trans. Alan Bass (Chicago: University of Chicago Press, 1982), 207–71.

57. See Chaim Perelman and Lucy Olbrechts-Tyteca, *The New Rhetoric: A Treatise on Argumentation* (Notre Dame, Ind.: University of Notre Dame Press, 1969), especially 1–10 and 510–14. Mailloux discusses the rhetorical force of New Critical scientism in particular and of theoretical appeal generally (4ff. and 150ff.). Once again Kenneth Burke's work was in the forefront; see *A Rhetoric of Motives*, 29–35. Foucault's analyses of Western science, particularly in *The Birth of the Clinic: An Archaeology of Medical Perception*, trans. A. M. Sheridan-Smith (New York: Pantheon, 1973) and in *The Order of Things* provide further warrants for including him in the ranks of the prorhetorical forces.

58. See the general analysis by Young, *Justice and the Politics of Difference*, 111–16. For specific manifestations of this exceedingly strong current in modern Western history, see Sheila Briggs, "Images of Women and Jews in Nineteenth- and Twentieth-Century German Theology," in *Immaculate and Powerful: The Female in Sacred Image and Social Reality*, ed. C. Atkinson et al. (Cambridge, Mass.: Harvard University Press, 1987), 226–59; Cornel West's chapter entitled "A Genealogy of Modern Racism" in *Prophesy Deliverance! An Afro-American Revolutionary Christianity* (Philadelphia: Westminster, 1982), 47–68; and Edward W. Said, *Orientalism* (New York: Vintage, 1979). The historical essays by a practicing paleontologist, Stephen J. Gould, also illustrate the sordid story of scientific racism and sexism. See, for instance, *The Mismeasure of Man* (New York: Norton, 1981); "Carrie Buck's Daughter," in *The Flamingo's Smile: Reflections in Natural History* (New York: Norton, 1985), 306–18; and "Science and Jewish Immigration," in *Hen's Teeth*

and Horse's Toes: Further Reflections in Natural History (New York: Norton, 1983), 291-302. The latter essay ends thus: "the [immigration] quotas barred up to six million southern, central, and eastern Europeans between 1924 and the outbreak of World War II.... We know what happened to many who wanted to leave but had no place to go. The pathways to destruction are often indirect, but ideas can be agents as surely as guns and bombs."

59. Hawkesworth, in *Beyond Oppression*, thus includes the "Rhetoric of Reason" (118-22) in her discursive typology; cf. Fuss. West writes that Martin Luther King's "universal and egalitarian and moral commitments... led him to *internationalize* the American ideals of democracy, freedom, and equality and thereby measure not only domestic policies but also U.S. foreign policy by these ideals"; "Martin Luther King, Jr.: Prophetic Christian as Organic Intellectual," in *Prophetic Fragments*, 12.

60. *Negative Dialectics*, trans. E. B. Ashton (New York: Continuum, 1973). In what follows I am indebted to the exposition of Young, *Justice and the Politics of Difference*, 98-121, and West's already cited chapter in *Prophesy Deliverance!*

61. Thus Emmanuel Levinas writes that we "do not need obscure fragments of Heraclitus to prove that being reveals itself as war to philosophical thought"; *Totality and Infinity: An Essay on Exteriority*, trans. Alphonso Lingis (Pittsburgh: Duquesne University Press, 1969), 21.

62. "In short, there is a growing nihilism and cynicism afoot in the country. This nihilism — the lived experience of meaninglessness, hopelessness, and lovelessness — encourages social anomie (drugs, crime) and therapeutic forms of escape (sports, sex). This cynicism... is a form of paralysis; the body politic shrugs its shoulders while it waddles in private opulence and public squalor"; Cornel West, *The Ethical Dimension of Marxist Thought* (New York: Monthly Review Press, 1991), xii. Dean's work also presents a thorough discussion of this trend in American intellectual circles.

63. I once heard West describe the necessity for "open-eyed optimism" in the work of social critique.

64. "Taking St. Paul Seriously: Sin as an Epistemological Category," in *Christian Philosophy*, ed. Thomas P. Flint (Notre Dame, Ind.: University of Notre Dame Press, 1990), 200-226. My argument here is greatly indebted to Westphal, but I question his exclusive concentration on the distorting effects of pride. In my view other tropes (sloth, disobedience) also have epistemological consequences. See chapter 4.

65. Quoted in Egil Grislis, "Calvin's Use of Cicero in the Institutes I:1-5 — A Case Study in Theological Method," *Archiv für Reformationgeschichte* 82 (1971): 15.

66. John Calvin, *Institutes of the Christian Religion*, ed. John T. McNeill, trans. Ford Lewis Battles, The Library of Christian Classics, vol. 20 (Philadelphia: Westminster, 1960), 1.5.14; 15.8, pp. 68, 196.

67. A point eloquently argued in Jones's *Critical Theology*.

68. It would be fascinating to compare the views of Calvin and John Henry Newman on this topic.

4. Rhetorical Hermeneutics and the Christian Doctrine of Sin Today

1. Merold Westphal, *God, Guilt and Death: An Existential Phenomenology of Religion* (Indianapolis: University of Indiana Press, 1984); Wolfhart Pannenberg, *Anthropology in Theological Perspective*, trans. Matthew J. O'Connell (Philadelphia: Westminster, 1985); Edward Farley, *Good and Evil: Interpreting a Human Condition* (Minneapolis: Fortress, 1991); Marjorie Suchocki, *The Fall to Violence: Original Sin in Relational Theology* (New York: Continuum, 1994; Ted Peters, *Sin: Radical Evil in Soul and Society* (Grand Rapids, Mich.: Eerdmans, 1994); and Cornelius Plantinga, *Not the Way It's Supposed to Be: A Breviary of Sin* (Grand Rapids, Mich.: Eerdmans, 1995). It is at least heartening to see something of a modest upswing in interest in the topic in the last two years.

2. This is true even of the far more numerous Roman Catholic contributions, though most are in the form of articles. Hormis Mynatty offers a valuable overview in "From 'Fundamental Option' to 'Social Sin': A Search for an Integrated Theology of Sin" (Ph.D. diss., Katholieke Universiteit Leuven, 1989).

Mention should also be made of more popular works by persons of various religious persuasions, such as Mark O'Keefe's *What Are They Saying About Social Sin?* (New York: Paulist, 1990) and Bernard Ramm's *Offense to Reason: A Theology of Sin* (San Francisco: Harper and Row, 1985). A few interesting contributions reflect the insights of psychology and recovery programs: M. Scott Peck, *People of the Lie: The Hope for Healing Human Evil* (New York: Simon and Schuster, 1983); Richard K. Fenn, *The Secularization of Sin: An Investigation of the Daedalus Complex* (Louisville, Ky.: Westminster/John Knox, 1991); and Patrick McCormick, *Sin as Addiction* (New York: Paulist, 1989).

In July 1993 *Theology Today* (vol. 50) devoted an issue to the doctrine of sin. The lead article by David Kelsey, "Whatever Happened to the Doctrine of Sin?" (169–78), argues that the subject hasn't disappeared but merely migrated into other doctrinal *loci*. But that, in my judgment, is simply a restatement of the problem. The rest of the issue offers interesting attempts to revive our doctrine from the perspective of various theological disciplines.

3. "Sin and Grace," in *Systematic Theology: Roman Catholic Perspectives*, ed. Francis Schüssler Fiorenza and John P. Galvin (Minneapolis: Fortress, 1991), 2:89, 102.

4. See the review by Mynatty, "From 'Foundational Option' to 'Social Sin,'" 81–157. One example of sustained hamartiological reflection may be found in Enrique Dussel's *Filosofía ética de la liberación*, 3d ed., 4 vols. (Buenos Aires: Ediciones Megápolis, 1988), vols. 3–4.

5. I am using a term suggested by Elisabeth Schüssler Fiorenza in *Jesus:*

Miriam's Child, Sophia's Prophet: Critical Issues in Feminist Christology (New York: Continuum, 1995).

6. In this respect the general scope of Suchocki's *The Fall to Violence* is particularly surprising, especially since she begins each chapter with a quote from newspapers reporting particular instances of evil.

7. (New York: Hawthorn, 1973).

8. See Edward Farley, *Theologia: The Fragmentation and Unity of Theological Education* (Philadelphia: Fortress, 1983); Van A. Harvey, "On the Intellectual Marginality of American Theology," in *Religion and Twentieth-Century American Intellectual Life*, ed. Michael J. Lacey (Cambridge: Cambridge University Press, 1989), 172–92; and William Dean, *The Religious Critic in American Culture* (Albany: State University of New York Press, 1994).

9. Mary Potter Engel, "Evil, Sin, and Violation of the Vulnerable," in *Lift Every Voice: Constructing Christian Theology from the Underside*, ed. Mary Potter Engel and Susan Brooks Thistlethwaite (San Francisco: Harper and Row, 1990), 152–64.

10. "Psychoanalysis and the Movement of Contemporary Culture," trans. Willis Domingo, in Paul Ricoeur's *The Conflict of Interpretations: Essays in Hermeneutics* (Evanston, Ill.: Northwestern University Press, 1974), 148.

11. *The Holy Family, or Critique of Critical Criticism: Against Bruno Bauer and Company*, trans. Richard Dixon and Clemens Dutt, in Karl Marx and Friedrich Engels, *Collected Works*, vol. 4, *Marx and Engels: 1844–45* (New York: International Publishers, 1975), 166–76. All emphases original.

12. In *On the Genealogy of Morals*, trans. Walter Kaufmann and R. J. Hollingdale, in a single volume together with *Ecce Homo* (New York: Vintage, 1969), 88.

13. First presented in *Beyond the Pleasure Principle* (1920), as discussed by Ricoeur, *Conflict of Interpretations*, 127–28.

14. *Gyn/Ecology: The Metaethics of Radical Feminism* (Boston: Beacon, 1978), 39. See also her broader assault on Christian hamartiology in *Beyond God the Father: Toward a Philosophy of Women's Liberation* (Boston: Beacon, 1973), 44–68.

15. "Gut ist: Leben erhalten und fordern; schlecht ist: Leben hemmen und zerstoren," in Albert Schweitzer's *Die Lehre von der Ehrfucht vor dem Leben: Grundtexte aus funf Jahrzehnten*, ed. Hans Walter Bahr (Munich: Verlag C. H. Beck, 1966), 32.

16. *Sin and Fear: The Emergence of a Western Guilt Culture, 13th-18th Centuries*, trans. Eric Nicholson (New York: St. Martin's Press, 1990), 5.

17. "Sin and Evil," in *Christian Theology: An Introduction to Its Traditions and Tasks*, ed. Peter C. Hodgson and Robert H. King, rev. ed. (Philadelphia: Fortress, 1985), 194–221.

18. For example, Haight, "Sin and Grace," 91–96; and Hendrikus Berkhof's *Christian Faith: An Introduction to the Study of Faith*, trans. Sierd Woudstra (Grand Rapids, Mich.: Eerdmans, 1979), 198–99.

19. See Daly, *Beyond God the Father*, and Elaine Pagels's critique of the Augustinian legacy in *Adam, Eve, and the Serpent* (New York: Random House, 1988).

20. *The Nature and Destiny of Man: A Christian Interpretation*, vol. 1, *Human Nature* (New York: Scribner's, 1949). He develops the contribution of Søren Kierkegaard.

21. *Man and Sin: A Theological View*, trans. Joseph Doncel (Notre Dame, Ind.: University of Notre Dame Press, 1965).

22. *Evil and the God of Love* (New York: Harper and Row, 1966). I question whether this view can be so easily attributed to Irenaeus of Lyon, since *Adversus haereses*, Hick's primary source, was written to counteract gnostic arguments against the goodness of physical creation. As the amount of space devoted to him in Hick's book shows, Schleiermacher probably deserves much of the credit for the formulation of this alternative. As the title of Williams's essay suggest, this theory tends to equate natural and human evil.

23. *The Symbolism of Evil*, trans. Emerson Buchanan (Boston: Beacon, 1967), and "'Original Sin': A Study in Meaning," in Ricoeur, *Conflict of Interpretations*, 269–86.

24. "The Rhetoric of Theological Argument," in *The Rhetoric of the Human Sciences: Language and Argument in Scholarship and Public Affairs*, ed. John S. Nelson, Allan Megill, and Donald N. McClosky (Madison: University of Wisconsin Press, 1987), 276. Klemm summarily dismisses "confessional" approaches.

25. Dean makes a strong case for the corrosive effects of poststructuralism on intellectual life in general and religious scholarship in particular; cf. Harvey's "On the Intellectual Marginality of American Theology."

26. Raymond Geuss, *The Idea of a Critical Theory: Habermas and the Frankfurt School* (Cambridge: Cambridge University Press, 1981), 2.

27. Thus even when he mentions the tradition of the seven deadly sins Williams states: "Such sins are not specific acts or deeds (or violations of rules) so much as they are structures of behavior and habits which serve the fundamental corruption of humankind" (215).

28. Cf. Ricoeur's concluding motto in *The Symbolism of Evil*, 347–57: "the symbol gives rise to *thought*" (emphasis added).

29. Richard Rubenstein, *The Age of Triage* (Boston: Beacon, 1983), 29–30. Of course the Iran-Iraq war, Operation Desert Storm and its aftermath, the Bosnian and Kosovar horrors, and genocide in Rwanda and Burundi have considerably increased this earlier estimate, though exact figures will probably never be available.

30. Lester R. Brown, "The Illusion of Progress," in Worldwatch Institute, *State of the World 1990* (New York: Norton, 1990), 11. In the same volume see also Brown and John E. Young, "Feeding the World in the Nineties," 59–78, and Alan B. Durning, "Ending Poverty," 135–53. Of course the inhabitants

of the Third World make up more than two-thirds of the human population of our planet.

31. The earlier warnings of Robert L. Heilbroner, *An Inquiry into the Human Prospect* (1974; New York: Norton, 1980) and William R. Catton Jr., *Overshoot: The Ecological Basis of Revolutionary Change* (Urbana: University of Illinois Press, 1980), once considered alarmist, are not easy to dismiss today.

32. "El D. F., al borde del desastre ecológico," *Visión*, 11 July 1988, 26–27. The situation in the world's largest city has grown steadily worse since this article appeared.

33. Cynthia Pollock Shea, "Protecting the Ozone Layer," in Worldwatch Institute, *State of the World 1989* (New York: Norton, 1989), 82.

34. "Bush Rejects Timetables on Pollution," a brief story buried on page A-11 of the *Atlanta Constitution*, 25 March 1992. The most recent round of global talks on environmental issues featured much lamentation about the lack of substantial progress in the last five years.

35. Potter Engel, "Evil, Sin, and the Violation of the Vulnerable," 152. The quote continues: "One out of every nine children under eighteen is abused or neglected by parent or guardian.... About 2,000 abused children die each year. One out of every three to five female and one out of every eleven male children will be sexually assaulted by the age of 19" (152–53).

36. Homicide is now the leading cause of mortality among African-American youths. There were 20,675 murders in the United States in 1988 alone. Carl C. Bell and Esther J. Jenkins, "Preventing Black Homicide," in *The State of Black America 1990*, ed. Janet Dewart (Washington, D.C.: National Urban League, 1990), 143–55; and Gerald Falk, *Murder: An Analysis of Its Forms, Conditions, and Causes* (Jefferson, N.C., and London: McFarland, 1990), 157.

37. The literature on this topic has become far too vast for citation here.

38. "On the Failure of All Attempted Philosophical Theodicies" (1791), trans. Michel Despland, in his *Kant on History and Religion* (Montreal: McGill-Queen's University Press, 1973), 283–97.

39. G. C. Berkouwer, *De zonde*, vol. 1, *Oorsprong en kennis der zonde* (Kampen: Kok, 1958), 5–19 (ET in one volume: *Sin*, trans. Philip C. Holtrop [Grand Rapids, Mich.: Eerdmans, 1971]).

40. In *Karl Marx: Early Writings*, trans. Rodney Livingstone and Gregor Benton (New York: Vintage, 1975), 423.

41. Leonardo Boff and Clodovis Boff, *Introducing to Liberation Theology*, trans. Paul Burns (Maryknoll, N.Y.: Orbis, 1987), 24–39.

42. In this book about rhetorical hermeneutics, then, I take exception to the sharp line Gareth Jones (*Critical Theology: Questions of Truth and Method* [New York: Paragon House, 1995], 110) draws between mystery/event and rhetoric, which he defines as "the real stage at which social and cultural concerns can and should come into theology." I believe our rhetorical sit-

uations also decisively stamp how we view and receive revelatory encounters and their textual expressions. Considering the reality of this give and take, contrary to many depictions I don't see such a chasm between the Chicago school of Gadamerians such as David Tracy, who stress how the situation alters one's perception of the text/narrative, and the Yale School of Wittgensteinians such as George Lindbeck, who stress how the text/narrative alters one's perception of the situation. I believe Francis Schüssler Fiorenza correctly includes both under the rubric of hermeneutical theology; "Systematic Theology: Tasks and Methods," in *Systematic Theology: Roman Catholic Perspectives,* ed. Francis Schüssler Fiorenza and John P. Galvin (Minneapolis: Fortress, 1991), 43–47.

43. I hope to return to socioanalytic mediation in a later work. I have already sketched possible directions for such a project in "Theology and Recent French Philosophy," an essay presented to the Pacific Coast Theological Society in March 1995.

44. W. Gunther Plaut, ed., *The Torah: A Modern Commentary* (New York: Union of Hebrew Congregations, 1981), 34–42. I thank my friend Ehud Ben Zvi for this reference.

45. *Summa Theologiae* 1.2, Q. 84, art. 1, in *Basic Writings of Saint Thomas Aquinas,* ed. Anton C. Pegis, 2 vols. (New York: Random House, 1945), 2:686–87.

46. See, for instance, his *On Wealth and Poverty,* trans. Catherine P. Roth (Crestwood, N.Y.: St. Vladimir's Seminary Press, 1984).

47. *Confessions* 4.2, in *Basic Writings of Saint Augustine,* ed. Whitney J. Oates, 2 vols. (New York: Random House, 1948), 1:42–43.

48. Extensive excerpts may be found in *Basic Writings of Saint Augustine,* ed. Oates, vol. 2.

49. Translated by P. Holmes, in ibid., 1:583–654.

50. Much depends on how one defines understanding. I argue that by defining this key concept primarily in terms of modern rationality, contemporary theology is pursuing a project different from that proposed by Anselm.

51. *A History of Christian Thought,* 3 vols. (Nashville: Abingdon, 1975), 3:120ff.

52. The study by W. A. Hauck, *Sünde und Erbsünde nach Calvin: Mit Berüchsichtigung der Sündenlehre Luthers und moderner Theologen,* 2d ed. (Heidelberg: Evangelische Verlag Jakob Contesse, 1939), represents a partial and inaccurate read of Calvin's thought. Readers interested in a more extensive version of my treatment here may wish to consult my forthcoming book, *Denouncing Death: John Calvin's Rhetorical Doctrine of Sin* (Lewiston, N.Y.: Edwin Mellen Press, 2000).

53. Cited in John Calvin, *Calvin: Commentaries,* ed. and trans. Joseph Haroutunian and Louise Pettibone Smith, The Library of Christian Classics, vol. 23 (Philadelphia: Westminster, 1958), 52.

54. A phrase used by Kenneth Burke, *A Rhetoric of Motives* (Berkeley: University of California Press, 1969), 99.

A Concluding Peroration

1. "Calvinism as Renaissance Artifact," in *Calvin and the Church: A Prism of Reform*, ed. Timothy George (Louisville, Ky.: Westminster/John Knox, 1990), 28.

2. Cf. Robert Schreiter, *Constructing Local Theologies* (Maryknoll, N.Y.: Orbis, 1985), 93–94. This view of catholicity is also developed in Justo González's *Mañana: Christian Theology from a Hispanic Perspective* (Nashville: Abingdon, 1990).

3. A term suggested by Ada María Isasi-Díaz, "Solidarity: Love of Neighbor in the 1980s," in *Lift Every Voice: Constructing Christian Theology from the Underside*, ed. Mary Potter Engel and Susan Brooks Thistlethwaite (San Francisco: Harper and Row, 1990), 33.

4. José Míguez Bonino, *Doing Theology in a Revolutionary Situation* (Philadelphia: Fortress, 1975), 100, 152.

Index